COOKING
IN THE LITCHFIELD HILLS

Designed and Illustrated
by PATRICIA and KERMIT ADLER

Published by
THE PRATT CENTER
New Milford, Connecticut

For Trudie Pratt MacDougall
who inspired us all.

Proceeds from the sale of this book go toward funding environmental education programs provided by The Eliot Pratt Education Center, Inc., also known as The Pratt Center, a non-profit corporation designated a National Environmental Study Area by the United States Department of the Interior.

Printed in the United States by
The Wimmer Companies
on Recycled Paper.

Additional Copies may be purchased by contacting
The Pratt Center
163 Papermill Road
New Milford, CT 06776
(203)355-3137
Cash, checks, VISA and MASTERCARD accepted

10 9 8 7 6 5 4 3

ISBN 0-9639175-0-1

First Printing   August 1993   3,000
Second Printing   October 1993   3,000
Third Printing   October 1994   3,000

The Cookbook Committee:
Judy Perkins, Chairman   Susan Rush, Vice Chairman
Lee Rush, Mary Jane Peterson, Sandra Daniels, Jolene Mullen
wishes to thank:

our Advisory Committee
for their time, counsel, expertise and love of this beautiful area —
Michael Ackerman, The Pantry
Hans and Kari Bauer, The Litchfield Wine Merchant
Dr. Paul DiGrazia, DiGrazia Vineyards and Winery
Lise Goedewaagen and Steve Levenstein, Food for Thought
Sherman P. Haight, Jr., Haight Vineyard
Ruth and Skitch Henderson, The Silo
Judy and Bill Hopkins, Hopkins Vineyard
E. Barrie Kavasch, Author, Food Historian
Carole Peck, Connecticut Catering Company
Susan G. Purdy, Author, "A Piece of Cake"
Adam Riess, Doc's
Arthur Schwartz, The Daily News/WOR-Radio
Julie Swaner, The Cobble Cookery

our Contributors
for sharing their thoughtful, delicious recipes that celebrate the bounty of
the Litchfield Hills

our Volunteers
for their eyes, ears, voices, fingers and favors —
Elizabeth Bontempi, Gretchen Farmer, Anne Marie Florio, Pat Garrity,
Dolores Hennessy, Joyce Henion, Gaye Parise, Karen Liebman, Celia
McTague-Pomerantz, Peg Molina, Kathryn Popper, Elizabeth Richmond,
Regina Perlowsky, Joanna Seitz, Judy Tabacinski, June Wildberger

Cathy Setterlin, Jane Uzwiak, The Pratt Center Staff
for patiently proving one computer and three offices can be shared like
loaves and fishes

and finally, Pat and Kermit Adler
for making us look good and making us laugh.

T hose of us who live in the Litchfield Hills know how lucky we are. We value the breathtaking beauty of this area — the sparkling air, the clear, clean water, the thrill of the changing seasons and the effect on all growing, living things.

Call it a fantasy life come true, if you will. On any given day you might enjoy such diverse activities as a polo game or a tractor pull. You could muck about in your garden by day, then party in grand style at nightfall.

There's a casual elegance to life in the Hills that is at once comfortable and civilized. So much natural beauty seems to bring out the best in everyone. You will see it in the way we cook. We love to prepare and eat delicious fresh food, especially food that is locally grown.

All proceeds from this book will go to The Pratt Center, an energetic non-profit organization. For the last 25 years The Center has been dedicated to bringing people closer to nature through community activities, school programs and a summer camp for children.

From frog pond frolics and wildflower walks, to community gardening and rock wall building workshops, The Center's 180 acre nature preserve is an exciting outdoor classroom. Science enrichment programs at over 60 schools extend our outreach to young people all over Western Connecticut. Each year The Center's activities enrich the lives of thousands of children and adults.

We invite you to celebrate our unique Litchfield Hills lifestyle as we share with you favorite recipes from our neighbors and friends.

Cathy Setterlin
Executive Director

Follow
The Pratt Center's
friendly frog
through these pages...
and STOP
wherever
your taste buds
take you.

Table of Contents

Anticipations

hors d'oeuvre, first courses and
accompanying wines to reward Mt. Tom leaf peepers
and Connecticut Wine Trail explorers
on their return home.

Grilled Pork Satés with Peanut Sauce

Chicken or beef may be substituted, but pork is the tastiest. Be sure to soak 16 bamboo skewers for 10 hours before using.

2 pounds pork shoulder or butt
For marinade:
$1/4$ cup lime juice
$1/4$ cup chopped scallions
2 tablespoons red pepper flakes
2 tablespoons soy sauce
1 tablespoon grated ginger root

1 large clove garlic, crushed
$1/2$ teaspoon salt
$1/2$ teaspoon sugar
For sauce:
$1/4$ cup creamy peanut butter
$1/4$ cup chicken broth
$1/4$ cup reserved marinade

Trim pork of most fat and cut into thin 2"x1" strips. Mix together all marinade ingredients. Reserve $1/4$ cup for sauce. Marinate pork in refrigerator 24 hours, turning several times. Skewer pork strips. Mix together sauce ingredients, and heat gently. Do not boil. Light grill. When ready, grill satés on all sides until browned, crisp and cooked through. Serve with warm sauce.
16 Servings

S. and L. Levenstein, Food For Thought
New Milford

Spicy Lime Shrimp

1 pound large shrimp, shelled and
    deveined
$1/4$ cup sesame oil
$1/4$ cup fresh lime juice
1 tablespoon minced ginger
3 scallions, minced

$1/2$ teaspoon dry mustard
$1/4$ teaspoon salt
Pinch crushed red pepper
Boston or bibb lettuce leaves
1 lime, cut into wedges

Cook shrimp in rapidly boiling water until just pink. Drain immediately and rinse under cold water. Combine next 7 ingredients and toss with shrimp. Marinate 2 hours in refrigerator. Arrange on lettuce leaves and garnish with lime wedges.
8 Servings

Pat Kennedy Lahoud
Bridgewater

Grilled Wild Mushrooms with Polenta

Best with a fragrant mix of mushrooms, such as oysters, shitakes, creminis and chanterelles.

1¹/₂ cups water
1¹/₂ cups milk
Salt and pepper to taste
1 cup yellow cornmeal
1 tablespoon sweet butter
¹/₂ cup grated Parmesan cheese
Bread crumbs

2 pounds assorted wild
     mushrooms, chopped
1 tablespoon minced shallots
1 tablespoon minced garlic
¹/₄ cup extra virgin olive oil, plus
     additional for sautéing
Fresh herbs for garnish

Combine water and milk in saucepan and bring to boil. Season with salt and pepper. Add cornmeal slowly in steady stream, whisking vigorously. Stir with wooden spoon until polenta starts to dry and pulls away from sides of pot. Adjust seasonings, add butter and cheese. Pour polenta onto jelly roll pan and spread to 1¹/₂" thickness. Let cool and cut into desired shapes. Dredge in bread crumbs. Toss mushrooms in bowl with rest of ingredients and season with salt and pepper. Put in hinged grill basket and grill until tender and golden brown. Sauté polenta in olive oil over low heat until golden on both sides. Place in center of plate and surround with mushrooms. Sprinkle with chopped fresh herbs.
6 Servings

William Okesson, The Boulders Inn
New Preston

Creamy Caviar Pie

3 ounces good quality caviar
8 ounces cream cheese
¹/₄ cup mayonnaise
2-3 teaspoons grated onion
1-2 teaspoons Worcestershire
     sauce

1-2 teaspoons lemon juice
Chopped parsley
1 hard-boiled egg, grated
1 red onion, finely chopped
Melba toast rounds

Rinse and drain caviar. Set aside on paper towel. Soften and blend cream cheese with mayonnaise; mix in grated onion, Worcestershire sauce and lemon juice to season. Spread in center of plate or tray in circle about an inch thick. Cover the top with caviar and the sides with parsley. Sprinkle egg and onion on top of caviar. Chill and serve with Melba toast.
8-12 Servings

Robin Leach
Danbury

Roasted Potato Skins with Scallion Dip

This is a great favorite.

4 pounds baking potatoes
Coarse salt to taste
For dip:
1 small garlic clove
$^1/_4$ cup chopped scallions
$^1/_2$ cup chopped, fresh parsley
    leaves

$^1/_2$ cup sour cream
$^1/_2$ cup mayonnaise
1 teaspoon Worcestershire sauce
    or to taste
Salt and pepper to taste

Preheat oven to 450°. Scrub potatoes. With paring knife, peel skin from potatoes lengthwise into $^1/_4$" wide strips, removing thin layer of flesh with each strip. (Reserve potatoes in cold water for another use.) Arrange strips in single layer, skin side up, on well buttered jelly-roll pans. Bake 15-20 minutes until crisp and golden. Toss skins with salt, transfer them to racks and cool. The skins may be made a day in advance, stored in airtight container and served at room temperature or reheated in a preheated 450° oven for 5 minutes or until hot. Make dip: in food processor mince garlic, scallions and parsley. Add sour cream and mayonnaise and blend until smooth. Blend in seasonings and chill in covered bowl overnight to allow flavors to develop. Serve with prepared skins.
6 Servings

Diane Sawyer
Bridgewater

Susan's Cheese Biscuits

The prepared logs can be held in the refrigerator several days before baking.

1 pound softened butter
$^1/_2$ teaspoon cayenne pepper
$1^1/_4$ cups flour
1 egg

1 teaspoon salt
1 pound grated sharp Cheddar
    cheese
1 beaten egg for egg wash

Mix first 6 ingredients together, adding grated cheese last. Be careful not to overmix. Form into logs about 2" in diameter, and chill. Preheat oven to 325°. Cut logs into $^1/_4$" slices; brush with egg wash, and bake until golden.

Michael Ackerman, The Pantry
Washington Depot

Seared Marinated Mushrooms with Chèvre Crouton

This is a great first course for a Litchfield Hills country dinner of grilled meat or fish. Use a mix of shitake, oyster and domestic mushrooms or, for the most interesting flavor, local wild mushrooms.

For vinaigrette:
1/2 cup peanut oil
1/2 cup olive oil
1 tablespoon balsamic vinegar
1 tablespoon cider vinegar
3/4 tablespoon white wine vinegar
Salt and freshly ground pepper to
    taste
For mushrooms:
2 ounces olive oil
12 ounces assorted mushrooms
2 cloves garlic, crushed

1/4 bunch fresh thyme
2 sprigs rosemary
Salt and freshly ground pepper to
    taste
2 ounces dry white wine
For garnish:
French bread, cut in 1/4" slices
Olive oil
Garlic, crushed
Chèvre or local goat cheese
Chopped tomato
Seasonal salad greens

Combine all vinaigrette ingredients and whisk until blended; set aside. Heat olive oil in sauté pan to just before smoke point. Add mushrooms, but do not stir until heat has recovered in pan. Sear mushrooms evenly. Add garlic, herbs, salt and pepper and continue to sauté. Add wine to pan, deglaze and reduce by 3/4. Lower heat, add vinaigrette and allow mushrooms to steep slowly. Remove from heat, remove herbs, and cool to room temperature. To serve, brush bread slices with olive oil and garlic. Toast in moderate oven until crisp. Top slices with chèvre and return to oven to warm slightly. Arrange greens on plate. Drain mushrooms, reserving vinaigrette. Scatter mushrooms on greens. Put chèvre crouton in center and top with some chopped tomato. Drizzle greens with vinaigrette.
2 Servings

Faith Stewart-Gordon, The Russian Tea Room

Harvest Country Paté

This paté has been with me in the Litchfield area a long time. Cornichons, whole grain mustard and a baguette make a classic accompaniment.

12 ounces pork fat, $^1/_2$" dice
2 pounds lean pork butt, $^1/_2$" dice
8 ounces chicken livers
8 cloves garlic
$^1/_2$ cup heavy cream
3 eggs
$^1/_2$ cup brandy
8 ounces cured ham, $^1/_4$" dice

8 ounces smoked tongue, $^1/_4$" dice
4 teaspoons salt
2 teaspoons white pepper
$^1/_2$ teaspoon allspice
$^1/_2$ teaspoon cinnamon
2 tablespoons Dijon mustard
$^1/_2$ cup flour
1 pound sliced bacon, divided

Preheat oven to 300°. Grind pork fat and pork butt fine with meat grinder into large stainless steel bowl. In food processor, purée chicken livers, garlic, cream, eggs and brandy. Mix into pork mixture. Add ham and tongue, mix well. Mix together next 6 ingredients and add to meat mixture. Line 2 terrine molds with bacon, then fill with pork mixture. Pack well. Top with bacon. Cover with foil. Bake in water bath filled $^2/_3$ way up molds for $1^1/_2$ hours, until meat thermometer reads 135°. Remove molds from pan, let cool and refrigerate overnight. Remove loaves by placing molds in hot water, then invert and tap out.
Yield: 2 loaves

Randy Nichols, Harvest Roasterie
Torrington

Roasted Red Pepper Dip

I met Jacques Pepin at The Silo and he was very helpful in assisting me to enter a Pastry Arts competition. He inspired this recipe.

4 tablespoons cilantro, chopped
2 cloves garlic
1 15-ounce jar roasted red
    peppers, drained
1 tablespoon sliced, pickled
    jalapeño peppers

1/3 cup almonds, toasted
2 tablespoons bread crumbs,
    toasted
1/3 cup olive oil
1/8 teaspoon salt
Crackers or Syrian toasts

Chop cilantro and garlic together in food processor. Add peppers, almonds and bread crumbs. Slowly pour in oil with machine running. Season to taste with salt. Serve with crackers or Syrian toasts.

Andrea Rush
New Milford

Meatballs in Cranberry Sauce

A healthy version of an old party favorite.

1 pound lean ground beef
1 egg white
$1/3$ cup bread crumbs
1 small onion, grated
$1/4$ teaspoon dried oregano

Oil for sautéing
$1/2$ cup low sodium cranberry
   sauce
Juice of $1/2$ lemon
2 fresh tomatoes, puréed

Combine first 5 ingredients and mix well. Roll into small balls. Brown in frying pan. Make sauce by combining remaining 3 ingredients. Add meatballs to sauce; simmer 30 minutes. Serve in a chafing dish.

Regina Perlowsky
New Milford

Lebanese Grape Leaves

Serve this appetizer, called Warek Eenab, at room temperature or as a main dish, with plain yoghurt, pita bread and tabouli.

100 fresh grape leaves, washed
1 cup raw rice
$1^1/2$ pounds coarsely ground lamb
   (not too lean) or beef

2 lemons, divided
Pepper, cinnamon, allspice to taste
1 tablespoon salt

Pour boiling water over grape leaves to soften. Mix raw rice, raw lamb, spices and juice of one lemon. Place 1 tablespoon meat mixture on veined side of each leaf. Spread across in a line, turn in the side ends and roll up completely. Line bottom of large pot with 3 or 4 unstuffed grape leaves. Place rolls evenly in rows and layer, crisscrossing each layer. Use inverted plate to hold down rolls. Add water to just cover. Bring to boil; reduce to low heat and cook 25 minutes. Add juice of 1 lemon 5 minutes before done. 8 + Servings

Pat Kennedy Lahoud
Bridgewater

Healthy Homemade Hummus

As a strict vegetarian, I select foods not only for taste, but also for nutritional value. Hummus is easy, tasty and rich in potassium and protein.

1 cup garbanzo beans, cooked until tender
1/2 cup of water
Juice of 3 lemons
1 cup of tahini (sesame paste)
1-3 garlic cloves, crushed
Pinch of sea salt
1/4 cup olive oil
For garnish:
1/4 teaspoon dried chervil or chopped parsley
Paprika

In blender, mix garbanzos, water and lemon juice until smooth, dip consistency. Add tahini, garlic, salt. Mix until smooth. Pour into a dip dish. Place dish in refrigerator for a couple of hours. At time of serving, add 1/4 cup of olive oil and a generous amount of freshly squeezed lemon juice. Garnish with finely chopped chervil and sprinkle with paprika.

Paul Winter
Litchfield

Crabmeat Indienne

6 baked patty shells, tops removed
6 tablespoons butter, divided
2 tablespoons chopped onions
1/2 pound mushrooms, coarsely chopped
Salt and pepper to taste
4 tablespoons flour
3 teaspoons curry powder
2 1/2 cups chicken broth
2 7 1/2-ounce cans crabmeat, flaked

Melt 2 tablespoons of butter over medium heat in saucepan. Sauté onions until soft and transparent. Add remaining butter, then mushrooms and sauté 3 minutes. Lower heat, sprinkle with salt and pepper; add flour mixed with curry powder. Blend. Add chicken broth, small amount at a time, and cook, stirring constantly until smooth and medium thick. Gently stir in crabmeat; heat 5 minutes. Spoon into warm patty shells; top with pastry tops and serve.
6 Servings

Lorraine Budny
South Kent

Brie with Fresh Cranberry Sauce

A synthesis of tart and creamy tastes. The jewel-like cranberries look festive on a holiday table.

²/₃ cup homemade cranberry
   sauce
4 tablespoons packed brown sugar
¹/₂ teaspoon orange liqueur
¹/₄ teaspoon ground nutmeg

4 tablespoons chopped pecans
Zest from 1 orange, chopped
1 small (15 oz.) Brie cheese
Melba toasts

Combine all ingredients except cheese and Melba toasts. Mix well. Peel top rind off Brie, leaving ¹/₄" rim. Top with cranberry mixture. Bake at 500° for 4-5 minutes, watching carefully so cheese does not lose its shape. Serve with plain Melba toasts.

Pegg Malone
New Milford

Colorful Shrimp Spread

8 ounces cream cheese
1 bottle chili sauce
¹/₂ pound cooked, shelled shrimp,
   chopped
1 cup chopped green pepper

6 scallions, chopped
1 cup ripe chopped olives
1 cup shredded mozzarella cheese
Watercress sprigs
Crackers

Soften cream cheese; spread in 9" circle on serving plate. Layer remaining ingredients in order on top of cheese. Surround circle with watercress sprigs. Serve with crackers.

Barbara DiGrazia, DiGrazia Vineyards
Brookfield

Lady Fisher's First Course

Guests have been known to secretly raid the refrigerator looking for leftovers as a midnight snack. A caviar garnish (domestic is fine) adds extra flavor.

8 ounces cream cheese, softened
1 can consommé, divided
1 teaspoon curry powder

Black pepper to taste
Parsley or caviar

Place cream cheese in food processor or mixing bowl. Add seasonings and ²/₃ can consommé. Process until smooth. Place in small ramekins and refrigerate until firm. Pour remaining consommé on each ramekin and chill. Garnish with parsley or caviar.
5 Servings

Jean W. Barlow
New Milford

Mixed Greens Spanakopita

A good recipe to double or triple for a party — it's always popular. The trick is to cook the liquid out of the greens without overcooking.

$^1/_4$ cup olive oil
$^1/_2$ cup finely chopped onions
$^1/_4$ cup finely chopped scallions
   and tops (2")
1 pound spinach, finely chopped
1 pound chard or mixed kale and
   leeks, finely chopped
$^1/_2$ cup finely chopped fresh dill
$^1/_3$ cup finely chopped parsley

Pepper to taste
$^1/_3$ cup milk
$^1/_2$ pound feta cheese, finely
   crumbled
4 eggs, lightly beaten
$^1/_3$ pound butter, melted
12 sheets phyllo (less than $^1/_2$
   pound)

Preheat oven to 300°. In large heavy skillet, heat oil to moderate. Add onions and scallions; cook 5 minutes, stirring until transparent. Stir in spinach and chard, cover tightly; cook 5 minutes. Add dill, parsley and a little pepper. Cook, stirring, uncovered, 10 minutes or until greens have begun to stick slightly to pan. Transfer to bowl; add milk and cool. Add eggs and cheese slowly and mix. Line buttered 12"x7"x2" baking dish with half the phyllo leaves, buttering each with pastry brush. Spread greens mixture into corners and level. Spread remaining phyllo leaves on top, buttering each. Trim edges with scissors. Bake in center of oven for 1 hour until pastry is crisp and delicately brown. Cut into small pieces for hors d'oeuvres or larger pieces for main course.
6-8 Servings

Vera Pratt

Radishes and Scallions with Avocado-Horseradish Dip

This will keep for a long time on the buffet if you place the bowl in a larger bowl of chopped ice.

5 tablespoons half and half
2 tablespoons lemon juice
2 teaspoons Dijon mustard
10 drops hot pepper sauce

1 ripe avocado, seeded, peeled
   and sliced
2 teaspoons prepared horseradish
2 bunches radishes, trimmed
2 bunches scallions, trimmed

Combine first 4 ingredients in food processor or blender. Process 30 seconds. Add avocado 1 slice at a time, pulsing each time, until smooth. Add horseradish and serve as a dip for the vegetables.
8 Servings

Ruth and Skitch Henderson, The Silo
New Milford

Potato Pancakes and Smoked Salmon Tartare

1 pound smoked salmon, finely
  chopped
2 tablespoons olive oil
1 tablespoon Dijon mustard
2 tablespoons capers
2 tablespoons chopped hard-
  boiled egg
2 tablespoons chopped parsley
2 tablespoons chopped red onion

For pancakes:
4 Red Bliss potatoes, unpeeled
  and shredded
1 egg yolk
2 tablespoons flour
1 tablespoon minced shallot
1 tablespoon chopped chives
2 tablespoons vegetable oil
Additional capers, onion, chopped
  egg and sour cream for
  garnish

Combine first 7 ingredients in mixing bowl and chill. For pancakes, combine next 5 ingredients. Heat oil in 10" skillet over high heat and drop potato mixture onto surface to make 1" round pancakes. Sauté until golden brown on both sides. On first third of each of 4 hors d'oeuvre plates, put $1/4$ of the pancakes, overlapping slightly. On next third of plate, put $1/4$ of the salmon, on final third, put 1 teaspoon of each of the garnishes.
4 Servings

**Tollgate Hill Inn and Restaurant
Litchfield**

A Taste of Summer

An easy hors d'oeuvre; I make lots of the basil purée in summer and freeze it in small containers for use throughout the year.

1-2 cloves garlic
3 cups fresh basil leaves
$1/4$ cup olive oil, plus or minus
1 loaf chewy French bread
  (2"-3" in diameter)
Olive oil for brushing

2 cups grated cheese (mozzarella,
  Parmesan, Romano or a
  mixture)
Toppings: sundried tomato, fresh
  diced tomato, minced onion,
  capers, black olives

Preheat oven to 375°. In food processor, mince garlic. Add basil, pulsing to chop. With motor running, gradually add enough olive oil to make a spreadable paste. Cut bread into $1/2$" slices and brush both sides with oil. Bake on cookie sheet, turning until lightly brown on both sides. Remove from oven. Spread each slice with purée. Top with grated cheese and sprinkle with assorted toppings. Return to oven and bake until cheese melts. Run under broiler to brown, if desired.

**Susan Eanes
New Milford**

Fig, Prosciutto and Cucumber Kabobs

As a caterer, I'm always looking for great tasting food that's quick to make, easy to eat and lovely to look at.

8 dried Mission figs
$1/2$ cup boiling water
8 paper-thin slices lemon, halved

16 thin slices kirby cucumber
16 (1"x 2") thin pieces prosciutto
    (about 2 ounces)

Cut figs in lengthwise halves and place in small bowl. Pour boiling water over and let stand 30 minutes to plump; drain. On 16 (6") bamboo skewers, thread 3 fig pieces alternately with 1 piece each of lemon, cucumber, and prosciutto.
16 Servings

Jean Galton
Sherman

Peanut Butter Sticks

These goodies keep so well in the freezer or fridge that it's worthwhile making an extended supply.

1 loaf firm, sliced white bread
1 12-ounce jar smooth peanut
    butter
$3/4$ cup vegetable oil

1 teaspoon sugar
$1/2$ medium-sized jar of peanuts
Salt, optional

Preheat oven to 250°. Cut crusts off bread slices and arrange crusts on baking sheet. Cut each bread slice into 7 strips and arrange on second baking sheet. Bake crusts and strips, turning occasionally until completely crisp, about 45 minutes. In blender or food processor, pulse crusts with peanuts to make fine crumb mixture. Empty into pie plate. In top of double-boiler over medium heat, combine peanut butter, oil and sugar. Heat through. Dip bread strips in warm mixture, then roll in crumbs. Store in air-tight containers.

Betsy Sands
Bantam

Crispy Cheese Crackers

Very simple, always tasty.

1 stick soft butter
1 cup flour
1 cup grated Cheddar cheese

1 cup Rice Krispies
Dash of cayenne pepper, optional

Preheat oven to 350°. Mix all ingredients together and shape into 1¹/₂" patties. Bake on cookie sheet until slightly brown on edges, 10-15 minutes. Store in airtight tin.
Yield: About 20 crackers

Elizabeth MacDonald
Bridgewater

Zucchini Squares

A great way to use all that zucchini! Serve as an appetizer or side dish.

3 cups coarsely grated zucchini,
   seeds removed
1 large onion, chopped fine
1 garlic clove, minced
¹/₂ pound extra sharp Cheddar
   cheese, grated

4 eggs, beaten
1 stick butter
1 cup Bisquick
¹/₂ teaspoon marjoram
Salt and pepper, if needed

Preheat oven to 350°. Combine all ingredients and place in greased 9"x11" baking pan. Bake 25 minutes. Cut into squares.
10 Servings

Carroll MacDonald
Bridgewater

"Spring Rolls"

Very pretty, very easy and delicious. These make an elegant party hors d'oeuvre.

40 thin stalks of asparagus
Large loaf dense, high quality white
   sandwich bread
Mayonnaise, preferably homemade

Salt and pepper
Fresh lemon juice
Pastel satin ribbons

Blanch asparagus. Trim crusts off bread. With rolling pin, flatten each slice of bread to thin it out. Spread mayonnaise on bread to corners. Put 2 spears of asparagus facing in opposite directions on each slice of bread so the head of each pokes out of the bread about 2". Sprinkle with salt, freshly ground pepper and lemon juice. Roll tightly and tie with ribbon.
10 Servings

Julie Swaner, The Cobble Cookery
Kent

Mushroom Caviar on Toast

Guests and family have complimented me on this easy and delicious appetizer.

2 pounds mushrooms, cleaned
  and chopped
1 medium onion, finely diced
2 tablespoons unsalted butter
1¹/₂ teaspoons freshly ground
  pepper

1 tablespoon tamari sauce
1 teaspoon (or more) dried thyme
2 tablespoons brandy
18 slices firm white bread
Unsalted butter to spread
Parsley sprigs for garnish

Over medium heat, cook and stir mushrooms and onion in butter with pepper, tamari sauce and thyme until most of liquid has evaporated. Add brandy and cook about 2 minutes or until liquid has evaporated. Adjust seasoning. Process finely in food processor. Chill and serve with baked toast. To bake toast: preheat oven to 350°. Remove crusts from bread; butter on both sides. Quarter diagonally and bake 20 minutes or until brown.
Yield: 3 cups

**Sally Williams
Washington Depot**

Creamed Mussels in Puff Pastry

8 pounds mussels
6 tablespoons shallots
3 tablespoons parsley
2 tablespoons chives
3 ounces butter
6 ounces white wine

Buerre Manié (mixed soft butter -
  flour)
4 ounces heavy cream
Salt and white pepper to taste
Puff pastry sheet
Egg wash

Pull off beards and wash mussels. Put in saucepan with next 5 ingredients. Cover and bring to boil. Simmer until mussels are opened. Remove mussels from juice and shell. Thicken juice with buerre manié. Cook 5 minutes. Add heavy cream; adjust seasonings. Pour sauce over mussels. Preheat oven to 400°. To make patty shells: make egg wash, then for each serving, cut 2 rounds of dough out of 1 pastry sheet with a 3¹/₂" cookie cutter. Now cut the center out of one of the rounds with a 2¹/₄" cutter. Brush full rounds with egg wash, place rings on top and brush tops with egg wash. Bake on a cookie sheet 20 minutes, or until puffed and golden. Cut lids out of centers of shells. To serve: spoon mussels into shells and crown with pastry top.
8 Servings

**Gérard Coyac, Le Marmiton
New Milford**

If you enjoy a glass of wine, here are some suggestions from our local, award winning Vineyards.

DiGrazia Vineyards & Winery

Fig, Prosciutto and Cucumber Kabobs	Vidal Blanc
Meatballs in Cranberry Sauce	Fieldstone Reserve
Mixed Greens Spanakopita	Anastasias Blush
Seared Mushrooms with Chèvre Crouton	Winners Cup
Susan's Cheese Biscuits	Autumn Spice
Colorful Shrimp Spread	Honey Blush
Creamy Caviar Pie	Vidal Blanc
Roasted Red Pepper Dip	Honey Blush

Haight Vineyard

Mushroom Caviar on Toast	Blanc de Blanc Sparkling
Spring Rolls	Covertside White
A Taste of Summer	Covertside White
Peanut Butter Sticks	Picnic Red
Radishes and Scallions with Dip	Barely Blush
Spicy Lime Shrimp	Blanc de Blanc Sparkling
Grilled Pork Satés with Peanut Sauce	Picnic Red
Potato Pancakes and Salmon Tartare	Recolte

Hopkins Vineyard

Crispy Cheese Crackers	Yankee Cider
Roasted Potato Skins	Chardonnay
Zucchini Squares	First Blush
Lady Fisher's First Course	Sparkling Wine
Healthy Homemade Hummus	Reserve
Crabmeat Indienne	Seyval Blanc
Grilled Wild Mushrooms with Polenta	Pinot Noir
Harvest Country Paté	Pinot Noir

Soup's on

beautiful soups to welcome back
Mohawk skiers, Hatch Pond skaters,
Waramaug sailors and
river rafters.

Fresh Plum Soup

This lovely burgundy-hued soup can be served warm or cold, as an appetizer or as a dessert. Use any fully ripe plums in season — Santa Rosa and Italian prune plums are two favorites. The number of plums is approximate depending on their size; have a few extra on hand just in case. Soup can be frozen, but darkens in color.

24 ripe Santa Rosa or 35 Italian
   prune plums
$^1/_4$ cup water or apple juice
2 tablespoons cornstarch
$^3/_4$ cup dry sherry or dry white
   wine, divided

$^1/_2$ cup granulated sugar
$^1/_2$ cup plain or vanilla low-fat
   yoghurt
Topping:
Additional yoghurt
Freshly grated nutmeg

Wash and pit plums but do not peel. Put plums in large saucepan, add water or juice and bring almost to boil. Immediately reduce heat and simmer about 15 minutes or until plums are fork-soft. Transfer all to food processor. Set saucepan aside but do not wash. Purée plums until pieces of skin are no more than $^1/_8$" across, you should have 4 cups purée. Return purée to saucepan. Stir cornstarch into $^1/_2$ cup sherry or wine, dissolving completely. Stir mixture into plum purée; add sugar and yoghurt. Cook over medium heat, whisking occasionally, for 5-7 minutes until thick and smooth. Add remaining wine or sherry. Taste and adjust flavor. Serve hot or chilled, topped with yoghurt and nutmeg.
6-8 Servings

Susan G. Purdy
Roxbury

Chilled Cucumber Soup

32 ounces plain, whole milk
   yoghurt
2 large cucumbers, peeled, seeded
   and chopped fine
2 cloves garlic, minced

4 cups cold water
2 tablespoons fresh mint, chopped
   coarsely
Salt and pepper to taste
Mint leaves for garnish

In large mixing bowl, combine yoghurt, cucumber, mint, water and seasoning. Stir well using whisk. Chill in refrigerator. Garnish with fresh whole mint leaves.
4-6 Servings

Riad Aamar, Doc's
New Preston

Carrot Soup with Coriander and Chives

A tasty soup, easy to make, and good either hot in winter, or cold in summer. Especially yummy with sweet, homegrown carrots. You can substitute half and half for the heavy cream.

4 tablespoons sweet butter
1 shallot, minced
$1^1/2$ teaspoons ground coriander
4 cups chicken stock
$1^1/2$ pounds carrots, peeled and
  thinly sliced
1 large parsnip, peeled and thinly
  sliced

$1/2$ cup heavy cream
Salt and freshly ground black
  pepper
$1^1/2$ tablespoons chopped fresh
  cilantro
Fresh chives

Melt butter in heavy saucepan, add shallot and sprinkle with ground coriander. Sauté 2 minutes, stirring frequently. Add stock, carrots, and parsnip. Bring to boil, reduce heat, and simmer, uncovered, until vegetables are tender, about 45 minutes. Purée mixture in 2-cup batches in food processor, until smooth. Return mixture to saucepan. Add cream and heat through. Season to taste. Serve hot or cold, garnished with cilantro and chives.
4 Servings

Chris Ford

Fresh Spinach Soup

I crafted this recipe myself and everyone loves it. It's fast, easy and pretty. Use garden fresh spinach when possible. Best made on the spot!

2 large, loose handfuls fresh
  spinach, washed
2 cups chicken stock, preferably
  homemade

1 tablespoon sour cream
A dash of Lawry's Seasoned Salt

Put ingredients in blender; press button and there you have it! Presto — fresh spinach soup. Serve hot or cold.
2 Servings

Mary Harwood
Washington

Summer Zucchini Soup with Nasturtium Blossoms

Pretty and cooling on a hot summer day.

1 large onion, diced
1 tablespoon olive oil
2 cups chicken stock
4 cups zucchini, peeled, $1/4$" dice
$1/2$ teaspoon salt
1 clove garlic, minced

$1/2$ cup fresh celery leaves, chopped
$1/4$ cup fresh parsley leaves
Pepper or cayenne to taste
Nasturtium blossoms, for garnish

Heat olive oil in large skillet, add onion and sauté until tender. Do not brown. Add remaining ingredients, except parsley, and bring to boil. Reduce heat and simmer until just tender, about 5 minutes. Process in blender with parsley, in 2 batches, until completely smooth. Chill several hours. Pour into individual bowls and garnish with blossoms.
4-6 Servings

**Eartha Kitt
New Milford**

Chilled Minted Pea Soup

A wonderfully easy summer soup. Best made with fresh shelled local peas; frozen will do in a pinch.

$1^1/2$ tablespoons olive oil
5 leeks, trimmed and sliced
1 clove garlic, minced
6 scallions, trimmed and chopped
3 cups shelled fresh peas
2 tablespoons chopped fresh mint

$5^1/2$ cups vegetable or chicken stock
Salt and pepper
Plain yoghurt
Additional mint for garnish

Sauté leeks, garlic and scallions in olive oil until they are soft 10-15 minutes. Add peas, mint, stock and season with salt and pepper. Simmer soup, covered, for about 25 minutes, or until peas are tender. Purée soup until smooth. Taste for seasoning. Serve chilled with a garnish of mint and a dollop of yoghurt.
6 Servings

**Julie Swaner, The Cobble Cookery
Kent**

Cold Roasted Yellow Pepper Soup

A summertime favorite at Doc's. Pretty with great depth of flavor.

4 large yellow peppers
2 medium potatoes, peeled and
   diced
$1/2$ cup celery, chopped
$1/2$ cup leeks, chopped
$1/2$ cup carrots, chopped
2 tablespoons olive oil

$1/2$ cup white beans, cooked
2 bay leaves
3 whole cloves
8 cups chicken or vegetable stock
Salt and pepper to taste
Fresh Italian parsley

Roast peppers over gas burner or on heavy cookie sheet, under broiler, turning until blackened. Peel skin from peppers. Remove seeds and chop coarsely. In large pot, sauté next 4 ingredients in olive oil until lightly browned. Add roasted pepper, white beans, bay leaves, cloves and stock. Simmer over medium heat for $1/2$ hour, stirring occasionally. Season to taste. Remove bay leaves and cloves. Purée in food processor until texture is very fine. Chill several hours. Garnish with parsley.
4-6 Servings

Riad Aamar, Doc's
New Preston

Iced Garden Yoghurt Soup

This is a first-rate hot weather soup. Serve outdoors in easy-to-hold mugs.

1 bunch scallions
1 bunch radishes
1 green pepper
3 small cucumbers, peeled
4 ripe tomatoes
1 clove garlic
3 tablespoons olive oil
$1/4$ cup parsley, chopped

3 tablespoons fresh dill
1 tablespoon fresh tarragon
32 ounces plain yoghurt
$1/2$ cup tomato juice
$1/2$ cup light cream
$1/2$ cup sour cream
$1^1/2$ teaspoons salt
Freshly ground black pepper

Wash, stem, seed and cut vegetables into chunks suitable for the food processor. In batches, purée the vegetables, herbs and other ingredients, being sure there is a mixture of solids and liquids in each batch. Put each batch as it is processed into large bowl. Thoroughly mix batches together. Season with salt and pepper. Add 6-8 ice cubes. Cover and refrigerate, overnight if possible. Before serving, stir well, correct seasoning and thin with tomato juice or ice cubes if necessary.
8 Servings

Kathryn Popper
South Kent

Grilled Corn and Smoked Chicken Soup

Adapted from a recipe served at The Coyote Cafe.

3 ears corn on cob, husks on
8 cups chicken stock
6 tablespoons smoked bacon,
    $1/8$" dice
$3/4$ cup smoked chicken breast,
    $1/4$" dice
$3/4$ cup red onion, finely chopped
$1/2$ cup plum tomatoes, peeled,
    seeded and diced

2 jalapeños, with seeds, diced
$1/2$ cup cilantro leaves
$1^1/2$ cups $1/8$" tortilla strips, fried
    crisp
6 wedges lime
1 ripe avocado, cut into 6 wedges
$1^1/2$ cups sour cream

Soak corn, husks on, in deep pot water, 1 hour. Drain and grill over hot coals, 10 minutes, turning frequently. Cool, remove husks; cut kernels off cob reserving cobs. In large soup pot, bring stock to boil and then reduce to simmer. Add reserved corn cobs and simmer 10 minutes. Meanwhile, cook bacon until crisp. Remove cobs from stock and add drained bacon, chicken, onion, tomato, corn kernels and jalapeños. Simmer 5 minutes, add cilantro and remove from heat. Divide tortilla strips among serving bowls. Place wedge of lime and avocado in each and ladle in soup, with sour cream on side as garnish.
6 Servings

Joanna Seitz, J. Seitz & Co.
New Preston

Potato Mint Soup

Fast, easy and delicious, this soup was inspired by a Native American recipe. The cilantro gives it a South American flavor.

8 medium potatoes, peeled, cut
    into small chunks
6 cups water
1 tablespoon butter
1 tablespoon olive oil
1 cup chopped onions
2 teaspoons salt

Ground pepper to taste
2 medium cloves garlic, crushed
$1/2$ cup mint leaves, chopped
1 tablespoon fine corn meal
$1/2$ teaspoon fresh dill or cilantro,
    chopped

Cook cut up potatoes in water, partially covered, until tender, about 20 minutes. Cool to room temperature. Meanwhile, sauté onions in combined butter and olive oil in large pot. Add salt, garlic and black pepper. Purée potatoes in cooking water; add to onions. Add mint leaves and corn meal. Add water if necessary. Cover and simmer for 30 minutes or more. Serve, topped with freshly chopped dill or cilantro. Can be made ahead and frozen.
6-8 Servings

Venay Felton

Amanda's Big Bean Soup

A very simple soup that can be as bland or zingy as you like. It's hearty and most welcome in cold weather. A good recipe to make with children — they love to choose the beans.

2 cups mixed dried beans (use lots of shapes and sizes)
4 cups water
Salt and pepper
1 bay leaf
1 clove garlic, minced

1 carrot, peeled and minced
6 cups water
Add to taste (be creative):
   Worcestershire sauce, Liquid Smoke, Tabasco, steak sauce, crumbled crisp bacon, etc.

In 4 quart covered saucepan, heat beans and 4 cups water over high heat. Boil 2 minutes and remove from heat. Let beans soak in covered pot one hour. Drain beans, discarding liquid. Add 6 cups water, salt, pepper, bay leaf, garlic, and carrot. Cover and bring to boil. Reduce heat and simmer for $1^1/2$ hours, stirring occasionally. Add various seasonings and taste frequently. Beans absorb flavorings readily, so be prepared to keep adding seasonings if you want a zesty dish. The longer it simmers, the thicker your soup will be. Thicker is better.
6 Servings

Lewis Banci
New Milford

Butternut Squash Soup Naria

This soup is easy to prepare, pleasing to look at and can be made up to 3 days in advance.

1 medium onion, chopped
1 tablespoon sweet butter
1 butternut squash, about $3^1/2$ pounds
1 cup chicken stock

$2^1/2$ cups fresh apple cider
2 teaspoons ground cinnamon
Pinch of ground ginger
Salt and pepper to taste
$1/2$ cup sour cream for garnish

In small skillet, sauté onion in butter and set aside. Peel squash, remove seeds and cut into large cubes. In a 4 quart pot, bring squash, stock and cider to a boil. Add reserved onion and spices and cook for 20 minutes or until squash is tender. Purée soup in several batches until smooth. Strain into 2 quart bowl. To serve, reheat and garnish each portion with 1 tablespoon sour cream; sprinkle lightly with additional cinnamon.
4 Servings

Eleanor R. Leon
Kent

Turkey Vegetable Soup

After Thanksgiving dinner, this makes a great Sunday night supper with popovers and salad. Freezes beautifully and is nice to have on hand when someone needs "chicken soup".

1 roast turkey carcass	2 cups cooked turkey, chopped
8 cups water or chicken stock	1 28-ounce can tomatoes with
1 medium onion, chopped	juice
1 cup celery, diced	1 12-ounce can whole kernel corn
1/2 cup chopped celery leaves	3 cups tomato juice
1 bay leaf	1/2 teaspoon dried basil
2 parsley sprigs	1 large green pepper, chopped
Salt and pepper to taste	Cooked pasta (optional)

In large kettle, place carcass, water or stock and next six ingredients. Bring to boil, skim, lower heat. Cook slowly, covered, for two hours. Remove from heat, cool, and cut meat from bones. Strain broth and place in refrigerator over night. Next day, skim fat from broth. Add turkey meat, tomatoes, corn, and basil. Mix well, add tomato juice and cook slowly over low heat for 30 minutes. Add green pepper and cook 30 minutes more. Add pasta if desired.
8 Servings

Gretchen O'Shea Reynolds
New Milford

Ultra Rich Cream of Mushroom Soup

My family requests this soup for Thanksgiving dinner, but I serve small portions so they will have room for turkey!

1 1/2 pounds mushrooms, sliced	8 cups chicken stock
2 sticks butter, divided	2 cups half and half or milk
1/2 cup sherry	1/2 cup flour
White pepper to taste	

In stock pot, sauté mushrooms in 1 stick butter until moisture cooks off (about 1/2 hour). They will look shiny. Add sherry and white pepper while cooking off this moisture. Add chicken stock. Simmer, uncovered, and reduce to 1/2 original volume. Add half and half or milk. To make roux, melt remaining butter in saucepan and whisk in 1/2 cup flour. Cook mixture until lightly brown, giving it a nice nutty flavor. Add roux to soup, using wire whisk to thicken to desired consistency.
6-8 Servings

Gale Hoffmann
Sherman

Ravenhill Herb Farm Sorrel Soup

In keeping with the spirit of "Victoria" magazine, where I am a contributing editor, this green and white soup can be garnished prettily with purple chive blossoms.

4 cups sorrel leaves, lightly packed
4 cups spinach leaves, lightly packed
4 shallots or 1 medium onion, finely chopped
2-4 tablespoons sweet butter

2 cups chicken stock
1^1/$_2$ cups half and half
Freshly ground black pepper
For topping:
^{1}/$_4$ cup heavy cream
^{1}/$_2$ cup plain yoghurt
Chive blossoms

In large saucepan, combine sorrel and spinach with water that clings to freshly washed leaves. Cook over high heat until steam forms. Reduce heat. Cover and simmer 4 minutes until limp, stirring once. Drain. Purée and set aside. In large saucepan, sauté shallots in butter 3-4 minutes until soft. Add chicken stock. Bring to boil, reduce heat and simmer 5 minutes. Add puréed vegetables to stock, whisking constantly until smooth. Gradually whisk in half and half. Season with pepper to taste. Purée in two batches. Cover and refrigerate until well chilled, 8 hours or overnight. Make topping: in small bowl, gradually stir heavy cream into yoghurt until smooth. Stir soup well (cream will separate during chilling). Pour into serving dishes. Gently float spoonfuls of yoghurt mixture atop soup. Garnish with chive blossom petals.
4 Servings

**Gaye Parise, Church Street Trading Company
New Milford**

Grandma Branson's Vegetable Soup

An ideal and economical soup when garden is producing beyond your wildest dreams. Virtually anything you pick can be added to this soup. There are two secrets — the marrow bone and the pressure cooker! Both are a must! Freezes beautifully.

1 large marrow bone
2 quarts fresh tomatoes, peeled
    and chopped (canned may be
    substituted)
1 quart water
3 tablespoons barley
2 onions, chopped
2 cloves garlic, minced
1 cup celery, diced
1 cup carrots, diced
1 cup cabbage, shredded

$^1/_2$ cup green pepper, diced
$^1/_2$ cup string beans, diced
$^1/_2$ cup fresh soy beans
$^1/_2$ cup summer squash, cut up
3 tablespoons chopped parsley
1 tablespoon chopped basil
2 teaspoons chopped oregano
1 tablespoon salt
Freshly ground pepper to taste
2 bay leaves

Place all ingredients in 4-quart pressure cooker and bring up to pressure. Reduce heat and cook on medium 10 minutes. Remove from heat, and let pressure subside on its own. Remove bay leaf and bone, scraping marrow back into soup. Best made 1-2 days ahead. Serve in warm bowls. You may want to thin soup with beef or vegetable stock. I make it very thick, freeze it that way and thin upon defrosting. Takes up less room in a crowded freezer!
Yield: $2^1/_2$-3 quarts

Mollie Rush
New Milford

Roasted Tomato Soup with Basil Purée and Goat Cheese Dumplings

6 pounds vine ripe tomatoes, cored
12 cloves garlic, finely chopped
12 sprigs thyme, stems removed
8 ounces extra virgin olive oil, divided
2 large Spanish onions, diced

4 ounces olive oil
1 large bunch basil, stemmed and divided
1 quart chicken stock
Salt and pepper to taste
1 pound chef potatoes
1 pound local goat cheese

Preheat oven to 350°. Place tomatoes, hole-side-up, on rimmed baking sheet, sprinkling with garlic and thyme. Drizzle with 4 ounces extra virgin oil and roast until very soft, about 45 minutes. Cool. In medium-sized, non-aluminum stock pot, sauté onions in olive oil until translucent. Add tomatoes and half of basil and continue sautéing 15 minutes. Add stock and simmer 30 minutes. Purée mixture and pass through coarse strainer. Return to pot and season to taste. In food processor, purée remaining basil, then drizzle remaining 4 ounces extra virgin olive oil into purée until completely incorporated. Salt and pepper to taste. Quarter potatoes and cook in salted water until fork tender. Drain and rinse in cold water. Cool. Pass through food mill, using small die, or use food processor, taking care not to overblend. Transfer potatoes to bowl and fold in softened goat cheese. To serve: ladle soup into bowls and drizzle with purée. Form dumplings using a mini ice cream scoop, place in center of bowls and garnish with additional basil leaves if desired.
8 Servings

**Kevin Schmitz, The White Hart Inn
Salisbury**

Joanna's Santa Fe Stew

This savory stew is easy to modify to your taste. If you like it thicker, purée some of the beans; for a heartier soup, add more meat; for a spicier soup, add more chili peppers.

8-10 cups chicken stock
2 cups mixed dried beans (kidney, pinto, black turtle)
2 cups onions, chopped
3 cloves crushed garlic
2 4-ounce cans roasted diced green chili peppers
3 tablespoons butter, divided
1 pound chicken, boned and diced (optional)
1 pound turkey or pork sausage, sliced (optional)
1 pound large shrimp (optional)

1 tablespoon ground chili pepper
1 tablespoon ground coriander
1 tablespoon ground cumin
1 teaspoon each dried oregano, thyme, basil
1 bay leaf
1 16-ounce package frozen niblet corn, steamed and drained. Do not use canned.
$^1/_2$ cup dry sherry
2 cups fresh, chopped coriander
Sour cream

Cook washed beans in stock for 2-4 hours (until tender). Add more stock if liquid drops below level of beans. Stir occasionally. In 2 tablespoons butter, sauté onions, garlic, and chili peppers. Add chicken and sausage, sauté on low heat until done. Put aside. Shell, devein and sauté shrimp in 1 tablespoon butter until pink. Put aside. Add all spices to cooked beans and stock. Add chicken and sausage mixture. Cook on low heat for $^1/_2$ hour. Stir occasionally. Add corn and sherry. Add more stock if needed. Warm through; take off heat and cool. Refrigerate overnight. To serve, reheat. Add shrimp at last minute so they won't be chewy or tough. Salt and pepper to taste. Stir in coriander, garnish with spoonful of sour cream.
8 Servings

Joanna Seitz, J. Seitz & Co.
New Preston

Fresh Pumpkin and Crab Soup

This delicious soup makes a beautiful presentation when served in a pumpkin shell.

1 3-pound pumpkin
4 tablespoons butter
2 bunches scallions
3 cups chicken consommé
4 ears fresh corn, uncooked
$^1/_2$ cup heavy cream

1 teaspoon curry powder
$^1/_4$ teaspoon ground cinnamon
Salt and pepper to taste
1 pound lump crabmeat
Additional pumpkin, 10"-12" in
    diameter, hollowed out

Cut top off first pumpkin. Scrape out and discard strings and seeds. Scoop out flesh. Trim and chop scallions. In large, heavy skillet, sauté scallions in butter until softened. Add small pieces of pumpkin flesh and toss to coat with butter; cover and braise over low heat until tender. In a blender, purée pumpkin, consommé and scallions in several batches and pour into soup pot. Simmer briefly. At the last minute, cut kernels from cobs. Combine cream, curry, cinnamon and corn in blender. Blend, then strain and add to soup. Gently stir in small pieces of crabmeat. Correct seasoning. Serve in second pumpkin.
6-8 Servings

Oscar de la Renta
Kent

White Bean Soup

A healthy, satisfying soup. Garnish with parsley or cilantro and serve with garlic bread. Best made ahead to marry flavors; freezes well, too.

2 1-pound bags white beans
3 celery stalks, chopped
1 large onion, chopped
1 carrot, chopped
2 cloves garlic, minced
3 quarts water
1 tablespoon extra virgin olive oil
2 leeks, white part, chopped fine

2 small celery stalks, chopped fine
2 cups peeled, chopped tomatoes,
    fresh or canned
1 tablespoon soy sauce
1 tablespoon balsamic vinegar
1 teaspoon sugar
1 cup chopped parsley

Soak beans overnight and drain. Put beans and next 5 ingredients in 8 quart stock pot and simmer, covered, 2 hours or until almost tender. In a separate pan, sauté remaining ingredients in olive oil until soft. Add to beans and simmer, covered 45 minutes to 1 hour. Purée 2 cups beans and stir back into soup.
8-10 Servings

Grace Giusti
New Milford

Meaty Ukrainian Borscht

Strong beef broth and garlic, not sugar, make a true Ukrainian borscht delicious. Fresh root vegetables and roasted beets provide plenty of sweetness which is balanced by an acid edge of lemon.

2 pounds beef flanken or short ribs

3 quarts water

2 teaspoons coarse sea salt

1 medium carrot, scraped

1 medium celery root, peeled, $1/4$ cut out for broth, remaining cut in $1/2$" cubes

1 medium onion, unpeeled, stuck with several cloves

8 whole allspice berries

3 medium-large beets, without tops

2 tablespoons butter or vegetable oil

2 large onions, coarsely chopped

1 medium parsnip, peeled, cut into $1/2$" cubes

2 medium turnips, cut in $1/2$" cubes, or 2 cups chopped cabbage

1 large carrot, cut in $1/2$" cubes

2 medium potatoes, cut in $1/2$" cubes

$1/2$ teaspoon freshly ground black pepper

1 well-rounded tablespoon tomato paste

8-10 large garlic cloves, crushed

Juice of $1/2$ lemon, or more to taste

$3/4$-1 cup sour cream or yoghurt

3 tablespoons finely chopped dill

3 tablespoons finely chopped parsley

In 5-6 quart pot, bring meat and water to boil over high heat. Reduce to simmer and skim off foam. When foam stops rising, add salt, carrot, $1/4$ celery root, whole onion and allspice; simmer gently, partially covered for $1^1/2$-2 hours, or until meat falls off bone. Preheat oven to 400°. Scrub beets, wrap in foil and bake for an hour, or until just tender. Poke through foil with skewer to check for doneness. Peel beets; shred on coarse side of grater. When meat is very tender, remove, strip off bones, and cut into small cubes. Place in bowl; cover with foil. Strain broth. Rinse out pot. Place pot over medium heat, warm butter, and sauté onion 2-3 minutes. Add cubed celery root, parsnip, turnips and carrot. Sauté 5 minutes. Add strained broth, potatoes, and shredded beets. Bring to boil. Reduce to simmer, uncovered, for 10 minutes, or until vegetables are tender. Just before serving, while soup is simmering gently, stir in garlic and lemon juice. Remove from heat immediately. Serve piping hot in flat bowls with dollop of sour cream and generous sprinkling of parsley and dill.
6-8 Servings

**Arthur Schwartz
Cornwall**

White Corn and Sausage Chowder

Memories of the Pilar Cafe, near Taos, New Mexico.

3 tablespoons unsalted butter
2 cups chopped onion
2 tablespoons flour
4 cups chicken stock
2 large potatoes, peeled and cut
  into small pieces
1 pound hot Italian sausage,
  cooked and sliced thin
1 cup half and half

4 cups cooked white corn
4 tablespoons hot salsa
Salt and pepper to taste
Garnishes:
1 cup chopped tomato
$^1/_2$ cup black olives
1 cup Cheddar cheese, shredded
Jalapeños, optional

In large soup pot, melt butter over low heat. Add onion and sauté until softened. Stir in flour to make roux. Add stock and potatoes and cook until potatoes are tender. Meanwhile, cook sausage, drain well and set aside. Add to soup the half and half, corn, salsa, salt and pepper to taste and simmer 7 minutes, stirring occasionally. Add sausage. Garnish, allowing cheese to melt slightly; serve immediately. Chopped jalapeños and more salsa may be added for those who want a hotter taste.
6-8 Servings

JoAnn Barwick
New Preston

Cream of Carrot Soup

Nutritious and easy. Serve it for lunch, or as a first course before a grilled fish entrée. It's a thick soup; if you prefer thinner soup, add more stock.

$2^1/_2$ tablespoons butter
2 cups carrots, scrubbed and
  diced
2 medium onions, diced
2 tablespoons flour
$1^1/_2$ cups degreased beef stock

$1^1/_2$ teaspoons salt
$^1/_8$ teaspoon pepper
2 whole cloves
$1^1/_2$ cups milk
Watercress leaves

Melt butter in heavy pot and when foaming, add carrots and onions. Stir and cook until onions are transparent. Add flour. Add stock slowly and stir until mixture is well blended. Add salt, pepper and cloves. Cover and simmer slowly for 30 minutes. Remove cloves and purée until smooth. Return soup to pot and add milk. Stir until it almost comes to a boil. Do not boil. Serve in warmed bowls and float 1 or 2 watercress leaves on top.
4-6 Servings

Alice Loebel
Sherman

Clear Beet Soup with Baked Mushroom Patties

This beautiful soup, called Barszcz is usually served with mushroom patties. It's a Christmas Eve tradition in Poland.

For soup:
3 carrots
2 celery stalks
2 parsnips
2 onions
5 peppercorns
Salt to taste
2 quarts water
6 medium beets
1 teaspoon dried marjoram
1-2 tablespoons lemon juice
1 teaspoon sugar
Dash pepper
For mushroom patties:
Stuffing:
2 tablespoons butter

1 onion, sliced
10 ounces mushrooms, sliced
2 tablespoons water
2 slices whole wheat bread
3 tablespoons fresh dill
Salt and pepper to taste
Dough:
$2/3$ cup butter
$2^1/2$ cups unbleached white flour
2 egg yolks
1 egg
3 tablespoons sour cream
2 teaspoons baking powder
1 egg white
Butter for cookie sheet

To make soup: Simmer first 5 ingredients in salted water 30 minutes; strain. Wash and boil unpeeled beets in small amount of water 30 minutes. Run under cold water, peel, grate coarsely, add to broth. Add marjoram and simmer 15 minutes. Strain. Add lemon juice and seasonings. To make stuffing: sauté onions in butter until golden. Add mushrooms and water. Cook on low heat 5 minutes. Soak bread in water; squeeze. Put everything in food processor, add dill, season with salt and pepper. Mix until creamy. To make dough: put first 6 dough ingredients into food processor and process until dough gathers into ball. Roll out 2 rectangles, 18"x16". Form line of stuffing 1" off one long side of each rectangle. Fold dough over stuffing, brush with egg white. Cut into 26 patties. Bake 35 minutes on buttered cookie sheet. Serve hot.
6 Servings

Teresa Bobbitt, Bobbitt's Health Food
New Milford

Hearty Chicken Vegetable Soup

A satisfying meal when served with Bob Fick's fabulous bread. Enjoy on a blustery day, or use as a cold remedy.

8 cups water
3 celery stalks, diced
3 carrots, diced
1 large onion, chopped
1 leek, sliced
1 turnip, sliced

2 parsnips, peeled and sliced
$^1/_2$ bunch parsley
$^1/_4$ bunch dill
2 bay leaves
Salt and pepper to taste
2 skinless chicken breasts, bone-in

Put all ingredients in pot and bring to boil. Reduce to a simmer, cover and cook 3-4 hours. After 2 hours remove chicken breasts, and vegetables, making sure no bones are left in soup. Remove bones from chicken, cut up chicken and return to pot. Additional water may be needed as soup cooks. When serving, return vegetables to soup. Flavor improves when cooked in advance.
8 Servings

**Robin Fuchs, Green General Store
Washington**

Salad days

fresh young salads to brighten
Kent Falls picnics, Washington Polo
hampers, luncheon or dinner
wherever you are.

Trout Salad with Endive, Radicchio and Mushrooms

1 head radicchio, trimmed and cleaned
1 smoked trout, skinned, boned and cut in $1/2$" strips
1 head Belgian endive, halved, cored and julienned
4-5 medium mushrooms, trimmed and sliced
3 tablespoons chopped parsley

4 sprigs parsley for garnish
For dressing:
2 tablespoons Dijon mustard
$1/2$ teaspoon finely chopped garlic
Dash salt and pepper
1 tablespoon fresh tarragon
$2/3$ cup salad oil
$1/3$ cup red wine vinegar

Set aside 4 large outer leaves radicchio for later use. Halve and core radicchio, slice into julienne strips. Set aside. In bowl, combine trout, endive, radicchio, mushrooms and chopped parsley. Mix dressing: place mustard and spices in food processor. Turn on, then pour in oil in steady stream while adding vinegar in three stages. Mix $1/2$ cup dressing with trout salad and arrange in center of radicchio leaves. Garnish with parsley sprigs.
4 Servings

S. and L. Levenstein, Food For Thought
New Milford

Ripe Tomato and Red Onion Salad with Roquefort Cheese

Wonderful made with produce from Henry Balsamo's. A perfect accompaniment with chicken pot pies or hamburgers.

3 large ripe tomatoes, peeled and sliced
8 fresh basil leaves, coarsely chopped
2 small red onions, sliced
Roquefort cheese, to taste
Salt and freshly ground pepper, to taste

For dressing:
$1/8$ cup extra virgin olive oil
$1/4$ teaspoon balsamic vinegar
$1/8$ teaspoon Durkee Bonne Saveur or Beau Monde seasoning
$1/8$ teaspoon freshly ground pepper
$1/8$ teaspoon Dijon style mustard

In large mixing bowl, layer sliced red onion on bottom, then add layer of sliced tomatoes, sprinkle with chopped basil and top with crumbled Roquefort if desired. Continue layering and end with tomatoes on top. Make dressing: combine all ingredients. Shake. Pour dressing over salad and serve immediately.
6 Servings

Phyllis McGloin
New Preston

Red Bean Salad

This salad, a great dish in any season, is from our cookbook, "Ruth and Skitch Henderson's Seasons in the Country". Of course, the "country" in the title, refers to our splendid Litchfield Hills.

1^1/$_2$ pounds dried red beans
2 bay leaves
1 teaspoon red pepper sauce, divided
^{1}/$_2$ teaspoon English dry mustard
Juice of 1 lemon
1 teaspoon honey
^{1}/$_4$ cup chopped fresh oregano

1 clove garlic, bruised
1 medium red onion, thinly sliced
4 small green Italian sweet peppers, finely sliced in rounds
Salt and freshly ground black pepper

Soak beans in water to cover overnight in large pot. Without draining, add bay leaves and ^{1}/$_2$ teaspoon red pepper sauce to beans and soaking water. Heat to boiling, reduce heat and simmer until tender, 1 hour. Drain and cool. Meanwhile, in medium-size bowl, combine mustard with a few drops water to form paste. Add remaining red pepper sauce and next 5 ingredients: whisk until thickened. Remove garlic clove. Combine beans, onions and peppers in large bowl. Add salt and pepper to taste. Pour dressing over beans and toss well. Serve at room temperature or refrigerate until ready to serve.
8 Servings

Ruth and Skitch Henderson, The Silo
New Milford

Springtime Watercress Salad

1 bunch watercress
2 cloves garlic
1 teaspoon anchovy paste

Juice of ^{1}/$_2$ lemon
1 tablespoon olive oil

Remove thick stalks from watercress, break leaves apart and put into refrigerator. Chop garlic very fine. Mix garlic with anchovy paste and add a few drops freshly squeezed lemon and 1 tablespoon olive oil. Rub dressing mixture into wooden bowl and, at last minute, toss watercress in mixture. Serve immediately.

Lisl Standen
South Kent

Roasted Potato Salad

Everyone loves this dish because it's simple and has lots of flavor. It goes well with hamburgers, grilled vegetables or chicken.

2^1/$_2$ pounds small Red Bliss or
    Yukon Gold potatoes
1 clove garlic, chopped
1^1/$_2$ tablespoons red wine vinegar
Salt and freshly ground pepper to
    taste

5 tablespoons olive oil, divided
1 tablespoon grainy mustard
2 teaspoons minced chives
1 teaspoon minced fresh rosemary

Preheat oven to 425°. Scrub potatoes; cut into quarters or if large, eighths. Put in single layer in baking dish. Scatter garlic, 3 tablespoons olive oil, salt and pepper over potatoes and toss. Roast 30-40 minutes, tossing gently every 10 minutes so potatoes will cook evenly. Beat vinegar and mustard in large bowl. Whisk in remaining olive oil until smooth. Add potatoes and mix evenly. Correct seasoning; cool to room temperature. Just before serving, fold in chives and rosemary.
6 Servings

Karen Valentine
Washington

Lemony Seafood Salad

For the best fresh fish, buy from the Maine seafood trucks which visit our towns toward the end of the week.

3 pounds mussels in shells
1 pound medium shrimp
2 pounds cleaned squid
^{1}/$_2$ pound sea scallops
1 bottle clam juice
3 bay leaves

^{1}/$_3$ cup olive oil
2 tablespoons oyster sauce
2 cloves garlic, crushed
2 tablespoons chopped Italian
    parsley
2 lemons

Clean mussels thoroughly. Place on rack in pan with small amount of water; steam until shells open. Cover shrimp with water; bring to boil. Turn off heat, let sit 5 minutes. Drain, shell, devein. Clean squid. Cook in clam juice with bay leaves 15 minutes. Drain, reserving clam juice. Poach scallops in clam juice 7 minutes. Drain. Remove mussels from shells. Cut shrimp and scallops into bite-sized pieces; cut squid into rings. Mix seafood together; add oil, oyster sauce, garlic, parsley and juice of 1 lemon. Slice second lemon thinly to garnish platter.
10 Servings

Mary Cortina
New Milford

Jack's Old Country Cucumber Salad

This salad, handed down by my mom, was always in a glass bowl on our Fourth of July table. It signaled the beginning of summer.

1 cup sugar
1 cup water
1 cup white vinegar
4 cucumbers, peeled, sliced paper
    thin
2 cups daikon radish, julienned

$^1/_2$ teaspoon ground white pepper
$^1/_2$ teaspoon salt
1 bunch dill, chopped
$^1/_2$ cup whole mint leaves
8 radishes, sliced

In large bowl, combine sugar, water, vinegar, cucumbers and daikon radish. Marinate 4-6 hours. Drain well. Add pepper, salt, dill and mint leaves. Just before serving, toss in red radishes.
8 Servings

Sandy Daniels
New Milford

Don Gaspar Salad

A tasty, mild accompaniment to a hot, spicy Tex-Mex meal.

1 16-ounce can whole kernel corn
1 16-ounce can pinto beans (or
    equal quantity home-cooked)
Homemade or good quality
    mayonnaise
$^1/_2$ teaspoon cumin powder
$^1/_2$ teaspoon dried oregano
1 small onion, minced

Salt and pepper to taste
2 large handfuls corn chips,
    crushed
1 cup grated Monterey Jack cheese
For garnish:
Additional corn chips and
    shredded crisp lettuce

Drain corn and beans thoroughly in sieve. Turn into bowl. Add mayonnaise to moisten. Add cumin, oregano, onion, salt and pepper to taste. Mix well. Before serving add corn chips, combining well. Top with additional corn chips, cheese and shredded lettuce.
4-6 Servings

Maggie Smith
Kent

Main Dish Summer Chicken Salad

2 cups real mayonnaise
2 tablespoons lemon juice
$2^1/_2$ tablespoons Chinese-type soy
  sauce
1 heaping tablespoon curry
  powder
1 tablespoon onion juice (or finely
  grated onion)
1 tablespoon chutney
3 cups chicken or turkey, cooked
  and cut into chunks

$1^1/_2$ cups chopped celery
1 6-ounce can water chestnuts,
  drained and sliced
2 cups seedless grapes
2 cups fresh pineapple chunks
1 $5^1/_2$-ounce package slivered
  almonds
1-2 tablespoons butter, melted
Salt

Mix together first six ingredients. Assemble all other ingredients, except nuts, and toss well in mayonnaise mixture. Place in refrigerator overnight so flavors blend. Just before serving, toast nuts in butter, then salt. Toss with chicken mixture.
8 Servings

U.S. Representative, Nancy Johnson
Sixth District

Shrimp, Orzo and Feta Cheese Salad

Cooling and colorful; a great supper or luncheon dish for a sultry summer day.

2 cups orzo, uncooked
1 cup crumbled feta cheese
1 large tomato, diced
$1/_2$ cucumber, peeled, seeded and
  diced
$1/_4$ cup diced red onion
2 tablespoons chopped fresh
  parsley

For dressing:
1 cup olive oil
$1/_3$ cup red wine vinegar
1 teaspoon minced garlic
Salt and pepper to taste
4 lettuce leaves
1 pound shrimp (about 16
  medium), peeled, deveined
  and cooked
Parsley sprigs for garnish

In large pot, cook orzo in boiling, salted water, stirring to prevent sticking, until al dente. Drain. Combine orzo, cheese, tomato, cucumber, onion and parsley. Mix together dressing ingredients and toss desired amount with orzo mixture. Divide orzo salad onto lettuce leaves and garnish with shrimp and parsley sprigs.
4 Servings

S. and L. Levenstein, Food For Thought
New Milford

Fernhouse Salad

2 teaspoons olive oil
4 teaspoons balsamic vinegar
$^1/_2$ teaspoon Dijon mustard
1 teaspoon garlic paste
1 tablespoon finely chopped
    parsley
Pepper to taste
4-6 romaine lettuce leaves, torn
    into bite-size pieces

$^1/_2$ red pepper, seeded and
    coarsely chopped
1 carrot, thinly sliced into rounds
1 celery stalk, thinly sliced
1 ripe tomato, coarsely chopped
3 tablespoons minced fresh basil
Pepper to taste
1 teaspoon olive oil

Beat together first 6 ingredients for dressing. Toss with greens, pepper, carrot and celery. Separately, gently toss tomato with basil, pepper and olive oil and arrange over salad. Serve with Fernhouse Pasta.
2 Servings

Patricia and Kermit Adler
New Milford

Tortellini Salad with Red Pepper and Salami Strips

This is a favorite for summer parties on our deck overlooking Candle-wood Lake. It looks great in a big red bowl.

12 ounces fresh cheese-filled
    tortellini
3 tablespoons red wine vinegar
1 tablespoon chopped fresh basil
1 teaspoon Dijon mustard
$^1/_4$ teaspoon salt
Freshly ground pepper

1 clove garlic, minced
$^1/_2$ cup olive oil
$^1/_4$ cup chopped fresh parsley
3 ounces salami strips
1 red pepper, cut in strips
2 tablespoons freshly grated
    Parmesan cheese

Cook tortellini according to directions; drain. Rinse with cold water; drain. Set aside. Mix together next 6 ingredients. Gradually beat in oil until blended. Lightly mix in tortellini, parsley, salami, red pepper and cheese. Cover and refrigerate 1 hour or longer to blend flavors.
4-5 Servings

Marguerite Malwitz
Brookfield

Salade Niçoise with Fresh Grilled Tuna

An updated classic, perfect for dinner on a hot summer night.

For vinaigrette:
1$^1/_3$ cups olive oil
2 tablespoons lemon juice
6 tablespoons balsamic vinegar
3 tablespoons Dijon mustard
2 small cloves garlic, minced
1 tablespoon minced fresh thyme
2 teaspoons minced fresh
    rosemary
2 teaspoons minced fresh oregano
Salt and freshly ground pepper to
    taste

8 small tuna steaks
Tiny green beans, whole
New potatoes, quartered
Ripe tomato wedges
Bermuda onion, thinly sliced
Bibb lettuce leaves
For garnish:
Hard-cooked egg quarters
Niçoise olives
Anchovies
Capers

Make vinaigrette by combining first 9 ingredients. Marinate tuna steaks in some of the vinaigrette for $^1/_2$ hour. Meanwhile, steam green beans until crisp/tender, then plunge into ice water to stop cooking and hold color. Drain. Steam potatoes (skins stay on better if quartered before cooking). In separate bowls, dress beans, potatoes, tomatoes and onions with vinaigrette. When ready to serve, grill tuna. Line 8 large plates with bibb lettuce; sprinkle lightly with vinaigrette. Slice a tuna steak crosswise and fan in center of lettuce. Using slotted spoon, arrange some beans, potatoes, tomatoes and onions around tuna. Garnish with eggs, olives, anchovies, and capers.
8 Servings

Nancy Kissinger
Kent

Orange Salad Italia

This recipe is refreshing, healthy and a unique combination of ingredients. Kids love it and can make it themselves.

8 large oranges
5 garlic cloves
$^1/_2$ cup olive oil

Fresh oregano, chopped
Salt and pepper

Peel oranges, break into sections, remove pith and cut sections in half. Peel garlic and chop very fine. Put oranges in bowl, add garlic, oregano, olive oil, salt and pepper and toss.
6 Servings

Pilar Miranda and John McNeely

Backyard Coleslaw

This light coleslaw is perfect for picnics since its vinegar base is safer for the outdoors. Make it one day in advance, but the longer it marinates the better it tastes. It will keep up to six weeks.

1 head green cabbage
4 small carrots
1 green pepper
1 small onion
$^3/_4$ cup white vinegar

$^3/_4$ cup water
$^1/_4$ cup sugar
2 tablespoons ketchup
Salt and pepper
Tabasco

Grate cabbage, carrots, peppers and onion together. Combine other ingredients and bring to a boil. Chill mixture and combine with vegetables. Use salt, pepper and Tabasco to taste. Let stand as long as possible.

Bruce Watts, Woody's B.B.Q.
New Milford

Sludge

I survived on this concoction for many years as a writer. My family's most frequent comment was: "Yuckck!!" It's fast. It's easy. It's horrible to look at. But it's really good, cheap, and you can live on it forever.

1 pint cottage cheese
1 piece fresh fruit of choice
1 small bag of potato chips
    smashed

1 California avocado, chopped
A few nuts of choice
Vinaigrette if you wish.

Mix in bowl. Do not look at it. Eat. Enjoy. Live forever. (Write five pages.)
1 Serving

William Kinsolving
Bridgewater

Unchicken Salad

This recipe uses tempeh, which is made from soybeans. We also use a tofu-based mayonnaise which can be found at your natural foods store. The dish is free of cholesterol and saturated fat, but still high in flavor.

16 ounces tempeh
$^1/_2$ cup tamari
$^1/_2$ cup water
1 teaspoon coriander
1 teaspoon garlic powder
3-4 tablespoons hi oleic safflower
    oil
2 carrots, diced

2 stalks celery, diced
1 red pepper, diced
1 medium onion, finely diced
1 medium bunch dill
2-3 large cloves garlic, pressed
$^1/_2$-1 cup tofu mayonnaise
Salt and pepper to taste

Mix together the water, tamari, coriander, and garlic powder. Pour into bowl and marinate tempeh 20 minutes, turning once. In large skillet, heat oil and sauté tempeh until lightly browned. Drain on paper towel and set aside. While tempeh cools, put vegetables in large bowl. Mince dill finely. Add to vegetables. Add pressed garlic. Cut tempeh into small pieces and add to vegetables. Stir in tofu mayonnaise, salt and pepper to taste. Chill.
6-8 Servings

Nancy Sherr, Chamomile Natural Foods
Danbury

Summer Strawberry and Onion Salad

Lovely for a barbecue, after a morning of strawberry picking in the local pick-your-own fields.

For vinaigrette:
2 tablespoons sugar
$^1/_4$ cup red wine vinegar
$^1/_3$ cup light olive oil
Few drops Tabasco sauce

For salad:
1 small head lettuce
1 cup sliced strawberries
$^1/_2$ medium red onion, sliced into
    thin rings
$^1/_3$ cup toasted sliced almonds

Make vinaigrette: stir sugar into vinegar until dissolved. Add remaining ingredients, stir well. Mix salad ingredients and toss with vinaigrette.
4 Servings

Manon Boucher

Cassoulet Salad

An easy main course salad with flavors reminiscent of the French classic. Great for using leftover leg of lamb.

1 large shallot, peeled and minced
2 cloves garlic, minced
2 tablespoons olive oil
4 1-pound cans white navy beans, drained and rinsed
3 medium-sized tomatoes, peeled, seeded and chopped
$1/2$ pound French garlic sausage, sliced $1/8$" thick
2 tablespoons parsley, chopped
2 teaspoons fresh oregano, chopped

$1^1/2$ cups Dijon mustard vinaigrette
2 cups julienne strips cooked leg of lamb, fat removed
1 whole skinless, boneless smoked chicken breast, cut in 1" cubes
For garnish:
1 head Bibb lettuce
1 ounce package sliced sundried tomatoes
Fresh basil sprigs

In a small skillet, sauté shallot and garlic in oil. Combine with next 5 ingredients in a large rectangular baking dish. Toss with vinaigrette to taste and marinate, refrigerated, 3-4 hours. When ready to serve, allow beans to come to room temperature. Toss in chicken and lamb and additional dressing to taste. Line a large bowl with lettuce leaves, spoon in salad and garnish with sundried tomatoes and basil.
8-10 Servings

Mary Jane Peterson
New Milford

Sunday supplement

it's breakfast, it's lunch---it's brunch, a Litchfield Hills tradition,
for city folk unwinding at bed and breakfast hideaways,
Sunday drivers exploring hidden roads, or for those
who are just relaxing with the big fat newspaper at home.

Fresh Corn Pancakes

This is a great way to use sweet corn slightly past its prime. If you want to serve these in the winter, the raw "creamed" corn can be frozen.

2 cups raw corn scraped,
   not cut, from the cob
1 egg, beaten
$^2/_3$ cup flour

$^1/_2$ cup milk
1 teaspoon baking powder
$^1/_2$ teaspoon salt
$^1/_4$ teaspoon ground black pepper

Be sure corn kernels are crushed so the corn "cream" is released. Stir all ingredients together, adjusting the milk and flour to preferred consistency. Cook on greased hot griddle.
Yield: 12 pancakes

Ethel Hurlbut
Roxbury

Asparagus with Scrambled Eggs in Puff Pastry

A taste of spring.

2 sheets puff pastry, (the size of a
   cookie sheet)
1 egg, beaten
16 whole large eggs
2 cups heavy cream or $1^1/_2$ cups
   crème fraîche

1 teaspoon salt
$^1/_2$ pound fresh asparagus spears,
   peeled
$^1/_4$ cup freshly snipped chives, or
   mixture of chives, tarragon or
   chervil

With 5" scalloped-edged cutter, cut 10 circles (make extras to allow for breakage). With 4" cutter, make indentation in center of each circle. Do not cut through. Carefully brush outer circle with beaten egg. Do not brush any egg in inner circle or pastry will not rise correctly. Place on cookie sheet that has been lightly greased or lined with parchment paper. Let rest in refrigerator at least 30 minutes. Preheat oven to 425°. Bake pastry 10 minutes until golden. Remove from oven. Remove inner circle, scooping out center to allow space for eggs and asparagus. Meanwhile, whisk eggs well. Add cream; beat 30 seconds until eggs are light. Add salt, pepper and herbs. Blanch asparagus in boiling salted water until just tender. Plunge into ice water to cool. Drain; cut into $^1/_2$" slices. Place large Teflon coated skillet over medium heat. (If necessary, cook eggs in 2 batches.) Pour in eggs and stir with rubber spatula until they begin to scramble. When cooked $^3/_4$ through, about 2 minutes, sprinkle on asparagus slices. Cook another minute until eggs are set but moist. (Cooked eggs can be kept in a 150° oven for 5 minutes.) Spoon eggs and asparagus into prepared pastry shells.
8 Servings

Carole Peck, Carole Peck Catering
New Preston

Genie's Puff Pancakes

This is a great recipe for a special breakfast or brunch. Use any fresh summer berries.

6 eggs
1 cup all-purpose flour
1 cup milk
$^{1}/_{2}$ cup sugar
$^{1}/_{4}$ cup fresh orange juice
2 teaspoons grated orange peel

1 tablespoon butter
$^{1}/_{2}$ teaspoon grated nutmeg
4 tablespoons butter
Fresh berries
Confectioners' sugar
Lemon slices and mint sprigs

Preheat oven to 450°. Place first 8 ingredients in blender and mix well. Put 1 tablespoon butter into each of 4 one-cup ramekins. Place in hot oven just long enough to melt butter. Pour batter into each hot ramekin and bake 20 minutes. When done, remove and cool 5 minutes or until puffs fall. Place berries on top and sift sugar over them. Place ramekin on small plate and garnish with lemon and mint.
4 Servings

Genie Munson
Newtown

Quick Spinach Soufflé with Cheese Sauce

This is the easiest and tastiest soufflé in the world. Excellent for brunch or dinner.

5 eggs
8 ounces cream cheese
1 cup skim milk
$^{1}/_{2}$ cup Parmesan cheese
One small onion
$^{1}/_{8}$ teaspoon nutmeg
1 package frozen spinach

For Sauce:
2 tablespoons butter
2 tablespoons flour
1 cup skim milk
$^{3}/_{4}$ cup Swiss cheese, grated
$^{1}/_{4}$ cup Parmesan cheese, grated

Preheat oven to 375°. Place first 7 ingredients in blender for 2 minutes. Put mixture into buttered and floured $1^{1}/_{2}$ quart soufflé dish. Bake 45 minutes, until top is golden and center is set. For sauce: combine butter and flour in saucepan and cook for 2 minutes. Add milk and cook until sauce thickens. Add cheeses and cook until they melt. Serve on top of soufflé.
6 Servings

Celia McTague-Pomerantz
Washington Depot

Good and Fruity Granola

4 cups rolled oats
1 cup shredded coconut
1 cup pine nuts or walnuts
1 cup wheat germ
$^1/_3$ cup sesame seeds

$^1/_2$ cup honey
$^1/_2$ cup vegetable oil
Raisins to taste
Mixture of pitted dates, prunes, or
    other cut up dried fruit

Preheat oven to 325°. Combine first 5 ingredients in large bowl. In small saucepan, combine honey and oil thoroughly and bring to boil. Stir honey mixture into oatmeal mixture, blending well. Divide granola between two 10"x15" baking pans, spreading evenly. Bake 25 minutes, stirring occasionally, until brown. Cool and add mixed fruit to taste. Store in air-tight container.
Yield: $1^1/_2$ pounds

Tom Brokaw
West Cornwall

Fabulous Tomato Pie

This is a famous and favorite recipe from the Chaiwalla Tea Room. Chaiwalla means "tea-maker" which is exactly what Mary McMillan does after choosing and importing nearly 30 varieties of tea directly from India.

2 cups flour
4 teaspoons baking powder
1 teaspoon salt
$^1/_4$ cup butter
Approximately $^2/_3$ cup milk
Ripe tomatoes, peeled

Salt and freshly ground pepper to
    taste
$1^1/_2$ cups grated sharp Cheddar
$^1/_3$ cup mayonnaise
2 tablespoons torn basil leaves
1 tablespoon chopped chives

Preheat oven to 400°. Place flour, baking powder and salt in bowl and cut in butter until mixture resembles coarse cornmeal. Add enough milk to make medium soft dough (not too soft). Turn about $^1/_3$ of dough out onto floured board and roll to fit 9" pie pan. (If dough breaks, patch it using scraps of dough and cold water.) Line crust with fairly thick tomato slices, sprinkle with salt and pepper, sprinkle with half the cheese and coat thinly with half the mayonnaise. Sprinkle basil and chives over mayonnaise. Add remaining cheese and spread mayonnaise over the top. Roll remaining dough thinly to fit over top of pie. Make slits to allow steam to escape, fit crust over top. Bake until brown and puffy on top, about 20 minutes.
6 Servings

Mary O'Brien McMillan, Chaiwalla Tea Room
Salisbury

Vidalia Onion Pie

This is wonderful with a salad and chilled white wine.

Pastry for single 9" crust pie
2 pounds thinly sliced Vidalia
    onions
1 stick unsalted butter

3 large eggs, beaten
1 cup sour cream
1 teaspoon pepper
$^1/_4$ cup Parmesan cheese

Fit crust into tart pan with removable bottom or 9" pie plate. Refrigerate. Preheat oven to 450°. Sauté onions in butter until tender. Mix eggs and sour cream in large bowl. Stir in onion and pepper. Pour into prepared crust distributing onions evenly. Sprinkle top with cheese. Bake 20 minutes, reduce to 325° and bake 20 minutes more.
6-8 Servings

Heather Herstatt
New Milford

Goat Cheese and Sun-dried Tomato Omelette

I developed this recipe using our own organic eggs, tomatoes and basil.

6-8 slices sun-dried tomatoes
5 large fresh eggs
1 tablespoon cold water
2 teaspoons olive oil

1 teaspoon butter
$^1/_2$ log chèvre cheese, crumbled
$^1/_8$ cup basil leaves, shredded

In small bowl, pour boiling water over sun-dried tomatoes to reconstitute. When softened, 10 minutes or less, drain and chop coarsely. Set aside. Preheat a 9"-10" omelette pan over medium high heat. Meanwhile, in medium bowl, beat eggs with 1 tablespoon cold water. Add butter and olive oil to hot pan. Butter will foam up; when it subsides, add eggs, stirring in circular motion with fork, lifting edges of omelette to let uncooked egg run underneath. When set, sprinkle cheese, tomato, basil, salt and pepper down center of omelette. Fold in edges to cover filling and continue cooking a few seconds longer to soften cheese. Slide omelette to edge of pan and flip onto a large plate. Garnish with fresh baby basil leaves.
2 Servings

Kathy Flynn, Sweetpea Organics
Washington Depot

The Best Buttermilk Pancakes

A Sunday morning institution. Folks come from far and wide to dig into these pancakes.

3 cups all-purpose flour
$^1/_4$ cup granulated sugar
1 tablespoon ground cinnamon
1 teaspoon ground cardamom
1 teaspoon baking soda
$^1/_2$ teaspoon baking powder

Pinch of salt
3 large eggs
1 quart buttermilk
$^1/_4$ cup vegetable shortening
$^1/_4$ cup butter
1 teaspoon vanilla

In large mixing bowl, combine first 7 ingredients thoroughly. In medium bowl, beat eggs and buttermilk together. Melt shortening in small saucepan. Cool slightly, add vanilla, then stir into egg mixture. Add egg mixture to dry ingredients, stirring until combined. Don't overbeat! Cook 5"-6" cakes on a hot griddle. Enjoy!
Serves a crowd

Dave Cadwell, Cadwell's Corner
West Cornwall

Pecan Belgian Waffles

Slices of warm, smokehouse ham make a tasty accompaniment to this Sunday brunch favorite.

$^1/_4$ cup Crisco
$^1/_4$ cup butter
$1^1/_2$ cups unbleached flour
1 tablespoon sugar
2 teaspoons baking powder
$^1/_2$ teaspoon baking soda
$^1/_2$ teaspoon salt

$^1/_4$ teaspoon cinnamon
3 large eggs, separated
$^3/_4$ cup sour cream
$^3/_4$ cup milk
$^3/_4$ cup pecans, finely chopped
$1^1/_2$ teaspoons grated orange rind,
    optional

In small saucepan, melt butter and Crisco and cool. Sift dry ingredients into large bowl. In separate bowl, beat egg yolks, sour cream and milk until smooth. Stir egg mixture gradually into dry ingredients, alternating with melted shortening. Stir in pecans and orange rind, beating until smooth. Beat egg whites until stiff peaks form; fold gently into batter. Bake in Belgian waffle iron according to manufacturer's instructions. Serve with pitchers of warm melted butter and maple syrup.
6 Servings

Mary Jane Peterson
New Milford

Summer Garden Zucchini Quiche

This quick quiche rises a bit like a soufflé. It's a delicious brunch or lunch entrée with a young green salad and sesame breadsticks.

Dough for 1 9" pie crust
1 medium or 2 small zucchini
4 ounces Swiss or Gruyère cheese
3 tablespoons freshly grated
    Parmesan
3 large eggs

$1^1/_2$ cups heavy cream
$^1/_2$ teaspoon salt
$^1/_8$ teaspoon nutmeg
$^1/_8$ teaspoon freshly ground
    pepper
2 tablespoons butter

Preheat oven to 350°. Line pie plate with dough. Shred cheese in food processor. Put aside. Shred zucchini. Distribute both cheeses evenly in pie shell; top with zucchini. Whisk together eggs, cream, salt, nutmeg and pepper. Pour over zucchini. Dot with butter. Bake 45 minutes or until set.
6 Servings

**Evelyn Portrait-Loeb
New Milford**

Easy Overnight Crunch

After the first time, you won't even have to measure. Bake it in the evening, then let it cool and crunch up while you sleep.

6 cups rolled oats
$^1/_3$ cup canola oil
$^1/_3$ cup brown rice syrup
$^1/_2$ cup Chinese pumpkin seeds
$^1/_2$ cup raw sunflower seeds

$^1/_2$ cup raw cashew pieces
$^1/_2$ cup shredded coconut
$^1/_4$ cup wheat germ
Pinch of salt, optional

Preheat oven to 250°. Spread oats in pan and drizzle with oil and syrup. (Brown rice syrup can be found at health food stores. It has a less sweet taste and adds crunchy texture.) Add other ingredients. Mix well and bake 1 hour stirring occasionally, until brown. Remove from oven. It will crisp as it cools.
12 Servings

**Cathy Setterlin
New Milford**

Eggs Fantastique

This is a perennial favorite at our Popple View Bed and Breakfast.

12 large eggs
$^1/_3$ cup sour cream
1 pound bulk breakfast sausage,
   crumbled
1 medium onion, chopped

$^1/_4$ pound fresh mushrooms,
   sliced
Salt and pepper to taste
$^1/_2$ pound Cheddar cheese, grated
$^1/_2$ pound mozzarella, grated
$^1/_2$ pound Swiss cheese, grated

Preheat oven to 400°. Beat eggs and sour cream together until thoroughly blended and pour into greased 9"x13" casserole. Bake 10 minutes or until eggs are just set. Meanwhile, in 10" skillet over medium high heat, brown sausage, breaking up large lumps. Drain thoroughly, reserving 1 table-spoon of fat in skillet. Sauté onions and mushrooms until softened; combine with sausage and spread gently over eggs. Season with salt and pepper to taste and evenly distribute grated cheeses over sausage mixture. Reduce oven temperature to 325° and bake 30 minutes or until cheeses are melted and slightly browned. Salsa makes a nice accompaniment.
8-12 Servings

Gretchen Farmer
Washington Depot

Eggs Italia

This recipe is easy, delicious, and beautiful for brunch. And it's so healthy when made with Litchfield County organic eggs. Serve with hot scones and a fine cup of Assam tea.

12 eggs
6 tablespoons pesto

6-8 slices ham
6-8 slices mozzarella

Preheat oven to 300°. Crack eggs into buttered 8" glass dish, sprinkle pesto, layer ham and mozzarella, and bake 10-15 minutes or until eggs are firm and cheese is melted. Serve immediately.
6 Servings

Mary O'Brien McMillan, Chaiwalla Tea Room
Salisbury

Danish Spinach Ring

For a show-stopping brunch entrée, fill the center with lightly sautéed cherry tomatoes, carrots, beets or shrimp.

2 pounds fresh spinach or 2-3
   packages frozen, chopped
$1/4$ cup heavy cream or milk

4 large eggs, beaten
$1/2$ teaspoon sugar
$1/2$ teaspoon salt

Preheat oven to 350°. Wash spinach and remove stems. In a large pot, steam spinach until just wilted. Drain and chop. If using frozen spinach, thaw in colander and squeeze out excess moisture. Return spinach to heat, add cream or milk and heat to simmer. (Do not boil.) Stir small amount of hot spinach mixture into beaten eggs and return to pot, blending well. Add salt and sugar and turn into greased ring mold, set in pan of boiling water. Bake until set, approximately 30 minutes. A knife blade inserted in the center will come out clean, when done. Turn out onto a platter and serve.
6-8 Servings

Maggie Smith
Kent

Bread: the rising art

Kent gallery goers and Cornwall campers
delight in freshly baked breads and muffins,
specialties from our kitchens, lovingly
recreated here for you.

Millstone Farm Maple Walnut Scones

Another good way to enjoy the local bounty using syrup from our own Connecticut maples. One dough ball may be frozen for later use.

3^1/$_2$ cups all-purpose flour
4 teaspoons baking powder
1 teaspoon salt
^{2}/$_3$ cup butter

1 cup milk
^{1}/$_3$ cup maple syrup
1 cup chopped walnuts
Additional maple syrup for top

Preheat oven to 375°. Mix first three ingredients in bowl. Cut in butter. Stir in next three ingredients. Knead on floured board six times. Divide into two balls. Place each on a cookie sheet. Flatten to about 2" and cut each into 6 wedges. Brush tops with maple syrup. Bake 15 minutes or until golden.
Yield: 12 scones

Avery Larned, Millstone Farm
Kent

Apple Pineapple Bread

We serve this at the Sanford Pond House, our Bed and Breakfast, which is a member of the Litchfield Hills Travel Council. It can be doubled and freezes beautifully.

3 cups all-purpose flour
2 teaspoons baking soda
^{1}/$_4$ teaspoon salt
^{1}/$_2$ teaspoon baking powder
1^1/$_2$ teaspoons ground cinnamon
^{3}/$_4$ cup chopped walnuts

3 large eggs
2 cups sugar
^{3}/$_4$ cup vegetable oil
2 teaspoons vanilla extract
1 8-ounce can crushed pineapple
2 cups shredded apple

Preheat oven to 350°. Combine first 6 ingredients in large mixing bowl and set aside. In another large mixing bowl, beat eggs lightly, add sugar, oil and vanilla; beat until creamy. Stir in pineapple with juice and shredded apple. Add dry ingredients, stirring only until moistened. Spoon batter into 2 well greased and floured 9"x5"x3" loaf pans. Bake 1 hour or until toothpick inserted in center of loaf comes out clean. Cool 10 minutes on wire rack before removing from pans.
Yield: 2 loaves

Charlotte Pond
Bridgewater

Carrot, Zucchini and Apple Muffins

Before becoming a restaurant owner, I baked these for the Bridgewater General Store. They were always a quick sell-out. A must for weekend guests; kids even love them. I usually have to double the recipe.

2 cups all-purpose flour
2 cups shredded carrots
1 cup sugar
1 cup shredded zucchini
1 Golden Delicious apple, cored
   and finely chopped
$^3/_4$ cup golden raisins
$^3/_4$ cup unsweetened shredded
   coconut

$^1/_2$ cup almonds, coarsely
   chopped
1 tablespoon cinnamon
2 teaspoons baking soda
$1^1/_2$ teaspoons grated orange peel
1 teaspoon vanilla extract
$^1/_2$ teaspoon salt
3 large eggs
1 cup vegetable oil

Preheat oven to 375°. Grease $^1/_2$ cup standard muffin cups. (These also make great mini-muffins.) Mix all ingredients, except eggs and oil, in large bowl to blend. In another large bowl, mix eggs with oil. Stir flour mixture into eggs. Spoon $^1/_4$ cup batter into each cup, peak batter in middle slightly. Bake until tester inserted in centers comes out clean, about 25 minutes. Serve warm or at room temperature.
Yield: 24 muffins

Kathleen Kinnison, La Tienda Café
Litchfield

Skiff Mountain Blueberry Biscuits

Skiff Mountain blueberries are a hallmark of Kent School.

2 cups all-purpose flour, sifted
$1^1/_4$ teaspoons salt
4 teaspoons baking powder
7 tablespoons sweet butter, chilled
$^1/_2$ cup milk

$^1/_4$ cup cream
$^3/_4$ cup blueberries
$^1/_3$ cup sugar
$^3/_4$ teaspoon ground cinnamon

Preheat oven to 425°. Resift flour with salt and baking powder directly into food processor bowl. Cut butter into 14 pieces and scatter over flour mixture. Pulse until it resembles coarse cornmeal. Transfer mixture into bowl. In a cup combine milk and cream. Make well in flour mixture, add milk mixture, stirring quickly and lightly until dough is formed. (No more than 30 seconds.) Gently incorporate blueberries, allow to rest 1 minute. Combine sugar and cinnamon. Turn dough onto floured board, pat gently into a circle, $^1/_2$" thick. Cut biscuits with $2^1/_4$" cutter and dip tops in sugar mixture. Place on lightly greased cookie sheet. Bake 10-12 minutes or until tops are golden.
Yield: 1 dozen

The Reverend Richardson Schell, Headmaster, Kent School
Kent

Challah

After our Holy Saturday Vigil, we break our fast by sitting down to hot cocoa and warm loaves of Challah. This recipe was given to us by our Subprioress' niece, Lisa Katz Elon, who lives in Israel.

1¹/₂ cups very warm water	2 teaspoons salt
¹/₂ cup margarine	3 eggs
6 cups flour, divided	¹/₂ cup raisins
2 tablespoons dry yeast	Oil
¹/₂ cup sugar	

Add margarine to hot water to melt. In separate bowl, mix 4 cups flour, yeast, sugar and salt. Add eggs and melted margarine mixture to form dough. Knead 5-10 minutes, slowly adding additional flour and raisins. Watch for blisters on dough; do not knead too much. Oil top; let rise in warm place 2-3 hours. Push down; let rise again. Do not over-rise or bread will be tough. Preheat oven to 350°. Shape and put into 2 greased loaf pans. Let loaves rise again 30 minutes. Bake 35 minutes.
Yield: 2 loaves

Reverend Mother Catarina Boyer, O.S.B., Abbey of Regina Laudis
Bethlehem

Simple Sour Cream Teacake

Not too sweet and a breeze to make.

1¹/₂ cups flour	2 eggs
2 teaspoons baking powder	1 cup brown sugar
¹/₂ teaspoon baking soda	1 cup sour cream
¹/₈ teaspoon cinnamon	¹/₄ cup melted butter
Dash salt	

Preheat oven to 350°. Sift first five ingredients together. Set aside. In separate bowl, lightly beat eggs. Add brown sugar, sour cream, dry ingredients and melted butter. Beat briefly. Pour into greased, 10" round pan. Bake 20-30 minutes or until toothpick comes out clean. Serve warm.
Yield: 1 10"cake

Kathleen Nelson
Gaylordsville

French Bread

I have taught many people, here and abroad, to make this. It's so easy, even a novice can serve home-made bread. No kneading required.

$^1/_2$ cup hot water or milk
$^3/_4$ cup boiling water
$1^1/_2$ tablespoons butter or
    shortening
1 tablespoon + 2 teaspoons sugar

2 teaspoons salt
1 package or cake of yeast
$^1/_2$ cup lukewarm water
4 (+ or -) cups unbleached flour
Lukewarm water to brush loaves

Combine first 5 ingredients and set aside to cool. Combine yeast and lukewarm water. Add to first mixture when it has cooled to lukewarm. Add flour to mixture. Stir well. Cover with damp cloth and set in warm (not hot!) area to rise until double. Preheat oven to 400°. Punch dough down, divide into 2 or 3 portions. Flatten each portion into long rectangle and roll up jelly roll fashion, sealing each turn by pinching and pressing down on dough. Place roll on greased baking sheet or into greased baguette pan. Make 3-4 diagonal slashes, $^1/_4$" deep. Cover with towel and let rise until double. Bake 15 minutes. Reduce oven heat to 350°, at same time, brush loaves lightly with water. Continue baking (30 minutes for 2 long loaves, 20-25 minutes for baguettes) and, 5 minutes before finished, brush loaves once more with water. The water creates hard crust. For shiny crust, loaves can be brushed with glaze of 1 beaten egg white mixed with 1 tablespoon water.
Yield: 2 long loaves or 3 baguettes

Kay Schaller
Roxbury

Nonnie's Peanut Butter Bread

My mother created this recipe. It is especially good when spread with butter and makes a nutritious snack or sandwich. It tastes best made a day ahead.

2 cups sifted flour
3 teaspoons baking powder
$^1/_2$ teaspoon salt
$^1/_2$ cup sugar

$^2/_3$ cup creamy peanut butter
4 tablespoons butter
2 eggs, well beaten
1 cup milk

Preheat oven to 350°. Sift together all dry ingredients. Work in butter and peanut butter until well blended. Add beaten eggs combined with milk. Mix thoroughly. Pour into well greased and wax paper lined bread pan. Bake 1 hour 10 minutes.
Yield: 1 loaf

Ruth Malins
New Milford

Mum's Oatmeal Bread

I grew up with the aroma of this Anadama-type bread wafting through the house. My mum made 10 loaves for my wedding and I always think of this as the inspiration for my baking career.

1 cup oats, quick or rolled
2 cups water, boiling
2 tablespoons butter
$^1/_2$ cup molasses

2 tablespoons yeast
1 tablespoon salt
4-5 cups flour (can be mixed white
    and whole wheat)

Steep oats in boiling water with butter and molasses for 1 hour. Dissolve yeast in $^1/_4$ cup warm water for 5 minutes. Add yeast mix to oat mix. Add flour and salt, a cup at a time. Dough should be stiff. Let rise, covered, in warm place free of drafts until doubled. Punch down, knead and divide into 2 loaves. Preheat oven to 375°. Place dough into 2 greased 9"x4"x3" loaf pans. Let rise, covered with tea towel in warm place until top of dough is slightly higher than top of pan. Bake 30-35 minutes until bottom sounds hollow when tapped. Cool bread out of pan on its side.
Yield: 2 loaves

Andrea Rush
New Milford

Honey Whole Wheat Bread

The wheat and honey harvest takes place in the fall at our Abbey in Bethlehem. I grind the whole berries as I use them. I try to make this recipe with our own thick, rich honey on a cold October day, hoping the kitchen will make pea soup or a white bean stew to accompany it.

1 cup milk
$^3/_4$ cup unsalted butter
$^1/_2$ cup honey
2 teaspoons salt
$^3/_4$ cup warm water

2 packages of yeast
3 eggs, broken up
5 cups unbleached flour
2 cups whole wheat flour
Soft butter

Heat milk and add butter, honey and salt. Mix well. Add yeast to warm water and set aside. When milk mixture is cool (not cold), add eggs and some of the flour. Then add yeast mixture and a good portion of flour until you have a somewhat sticky dough. (The barometer has more to do with the amount of flour than any recipe!) When it is fairly smooth, knead, not too much, and shape into two rounded loaves which then sit on pie plates to rise. When each has doubled in bulk, put into hot oven (375°). Right before they are ready to come out, about 35-40 minutes, rub them both with butter. This gives a shiny, tasty crust, soft but very dark and flavorful.
Yield: 2 loaves

Reverend Mother Catarina Boyer, O.S.B., Abbey of Regina Laudis
Bethlehem

Wonderful Wheat-Free Carrot Muffins

So delicious you'll never miss the wheat. Spelt flour can be found at your natural foods store.

2 cups finely chopped carrots
2 1/2 cups spelt flour
1/2 cup hi oleic safflower oil
1/2 cup currants
1/2 cup chopped walnuts
2 teaspoons cinnamon
1 teaspoon nutmeg

1 teaspoon allspice
1 teaspoon salt
2 teaspoons baking powder
1 teaspoon baking soda
3/4 cup maple syrup
4 large eggs

Preheat oven to 350°. In bowl of food processor, finely chop carrots. Measure two cups packed and set aside. In separate bowl, mix dry ingredients. In food processor, mix together wet ingredients and carrots. Process until well blended. Mix wet and dry ingredients until just blended. Do not overmix. Spoon mixture into well greased muffin tin. Bake 15 minutes or until cake tester comes out clean when inserted in center. Remove from oven. Allow muffins to cool in pan for 10 minutes. Remove from pan and cool on wire rack.
Yield: 12-18 muffins

Nancy Sherr, Chamomile Natural Foods
Danbury

Carrot Walnut Bread

This moist, satisfying bread is easy to make, healthy to eat, and freezes well. It's made with all natural ingredients.

1 cup vegetable oil
3/4 cup sugar
2 eggs
1 teaspoon vanilla
3/4 cup unbleached all-purpose
    flour

3/4 cup whole wheat flour
1 1/2 teaspoons baking soda
1 1/2 teaspoons ground cinnamon
1/2 teaspoon salt
1 1/2 cups grated carrots
1 1/2 cups chopped walnuts

Preheat oven to 350°. Grease and flour loaf pan. Combine oil, sugar, eggs and vanilla in large bowl. Sift flours, baking soda, cinnamon and salt into another bowl. Add to sugar mixture. Stir in carrots and walnuts, mixing just until blended. Turn into prepared pan. Bake at 350° 1 hour or until center springs back when lightly pressed with fingertip. Cool in pan 10 minutes. Turn out onto wire rack and cool completely.
Yield: 1 loaf

Laura Purbeck
Falls Village

Cloverleaf Farm Blueberry Cake

Make this wonderful coffee cake with fresh berries and serve it warm.

For Topping:
1 cup brown sugar
1 tablespoon flour
1 teaspoon cinnamon
2 tablespoons butter
1 cup chopped pecans
For Cake:
2 cups unbleached flour
1 teaspoon baking soda
1 teaspoon baking powder

$^1/_2$ teaspoon nutmeg
$^1/_4$ teaspoon salt
6 tablespoons butter
$^3/_4$ cup sugar
2 eggs
1 cup yoghurt or buttermilk
1 teaspoon grated lemon peel
1 teaspoon vanilla
2 tablespoons lemon juice
3 cups blueberries, divided

Make topping: in medium bowl, blend sugar, flour, and cinnamon. Cut in butter until mixture resembles coarse cornmeal. Mix in chopped pecans. Set aside. Make cake: preheat oven to 375°. In small bowl, mix flour, baking soda, baking powder, nutmeg and salt. In another bowl cream sugar and butter until fluffy and light. Add eggs, one at a time. Mix in yoghurt or buttermilk, lemon peel, lemon juice and vanilla. Add to dry ingredients, mixing only until batter is moistened. Fold in one cup blueberries. Pour into greased, non-reactive 9"x13" pan and spread evenly. Spread remaining 2 cups blueberries on top. Add topping. Bake on center rack of oven 50 minutes to one hour. Cool in pan.

Nancy MacGregor
Sherman

Jalapeño Cheese Cornbread

A customer favorite, it's a perfect partner for our pit-smoked barbecue.

4 cups all-purpose flour
2 cups cornmeal
$1^1/_2$ cups sugar
1 teaspoon salt
2 tablespoons baking powder
4 large eggs

3 cups milk
$2^1/_2$ tablespoons vegetable oil
$^1/_2$ cup melted butter
$^1/_2$ cup chopped jalapeño peppers
$^1/_2$ cup shredded Cheddar cheese

Preheat oven to 350°. Grease 12"x8"x2" pan. Sift dry ingredients into large bowl. Beat eggs, milk and vegetable oil in separate bowl. Add liquid ingredients plus melted butter to dry mixture, stirring until just blended. Add peppers and cheese, taking care not to overblend. Pour batter into pan. Bake 1 hour or until golden brown. Best served hot out of the oven.
12-15 Servings

Paul Haas, Woody's B.B.Q.
New Milford

"Quid"essential Blueberry Muffins

Guests at The Quid, my Bed and Breakfast, have dubbed these "killer" muffins. Pick the berries one day, indulge yourselves the following morning.

For muffins:
3-4 tablespoons chopped orange
1 cup buttermilk
1 large egg
$^1/_2$ cup butter, melted
$^3/_4$ cup sugar
$2^1/_4$ cups flour
1 tablespoon baking powder

$1^3/_4$ cups blueberries
For glaze:
$1^1/_2$ tablespoons orange juice
1 tablespoon lemon juice
$^1/_3$ cup sifted confectioners' sugar
2 teaspoons grated orange peel
2 teaspoons grated lemon peel

Preheat oven to 400°. In food processor, chop whole orange segments, peel and all. Combine with next 4 ingredients until blended. Stir in flour and baking powder until just moistened. Stir in berries. Put into greased 12 cup muffin pan. Bake 22-25 minutes or until toothpick comes out clean. Cool in pan. Make glaze: combine all ingredients; stir until well blended. Drizzle over cooled muffins.
Yield: 12 muffins

Susan Rush
New Milford

Holiday Date Loaf

This has been a Christmastime family dessert for over 100 years. My mother remembered shelling walnuts and pitting dates for her mother as a young girl. This bread should be thinly sliced and keeps well for weeks if tightly wrapped.

1 pound whole walnuts, shelled
1 pound whole dates, pitted
1 cup all-purpose flour
$^1/_2$ teaspoon salt

3 teaspoons baking powder
1 cup sugar
4 eggs, separated
1 teaspoon vanilla

Preheat oven to 250°. Grease 9"x5"x3" loaf pan and line with wax paper (very important). Put walnuts and dates into large bowl. Sift flour, salt and baking powder twice and then sift again over nuts and dates. Mix well. Add 1 cup sugar and mix well again. Beat whites and yolks of eggs separately, then fold together. Add 1 teaspoon vanilla. Add this mixture to first mixture and stir until no dry ingredients are visible. Bake 2 hours. Cool 1 hour in pan, then remove and enjoy!
Yield: 1 loaf

Marian W. Landig
New Milford

Glazed Cinnamon Buns

Wonderful for weekend guests and holiday breakfasts because the preparation can be done in stages the day before.

For dough:
1 package dry yeast
3 tablespoons sugar, divided
2 tablespoons unsalted butter
$1/2$ cup milk
$1^1/4$ teaspoons salt
1 large egg
3-$3^1/4$ cups all-purpose flour,
   divided

For filling:
$1^1/2$ tablespoons unsalted butter,
   melted and cooled
$1/3$ cup firmly packed light brown
   sugar
2 teaspoons cinnamon
$1/2$ cup raisins
For glaze:
$1^1/4$ cups confectioners' sugar
2 tablespoons unsalted butter,
   melted and cooled
2-3 tablespoons milk

In large bowl, proof yeast with 1 tablespoon sugar in $1/2$ cup warm water for 5 minutes. In small pan, melt butter; add milk, remaining 2 tablespoons sugar and salt. Heat to lukewarm. Combine yeast mixture, milk mixture, egg and 3 cups flour. Stir. In heavy duty mixer, knead until dough is smooth and elastic, adding up to $1/4$ cup flour if necessary to prevent sticking. (Or knead by hand 8-10 minutes.) Put dough ball in buttered bowl, cover; let rise 1 hour or until doubled. (Or let dough rise in refrigerator 8 hours or overnight.) Turn dough onto floured surface; roll into 12"x9" rectangle. Brush with butter. In small bowl, stir together brown sugar and cinnamon; sprinkle mixture over dough. Sprinkle on raisins. Starting with long side, roll dough jelly roll fashion. Cut into 12 equal pieces. Put pieces in buttered $1/2$ cup muffin tins. Let buns rise, covered, 45 minutes or until almost double. (Or let buns rise in refrigerator 8 hours or overnight and finish rising in morning by placing pans on top of running clothes dryer for 20-30 minutes.) Preheat oven to 400°. Bake 16-18 minutes or until golden. While baking, make glaze. Sift sugar into bowl; add butter and milk, whisk until smooth. Add 1 tablespoon more milk if necessary to make thick, pourable glaze. Pour glaze over buns while still warm from oven.
Yield: 12 buns

Jolene Mullen
New Milford

Mapley Apple Muffins

When these muffins are baking, you can smell the perfume of a New England fall. Like all the recipes in my new cookbook, "Have Your Cake and Eat It, Too", they're nutritious, filled with fiber and low in fat.

3 tablespoons canola or safflower
   oil
1 large egg plus 1 egg white
$^1/_4$ cup pure maple syrup
$^1/_2$ cup apple sauce, unsweetened
$^1/_2$ cup cider or apple juice
$^1/_2$ cup dark brown sugar, packed
$^1/_2$ teaspoon maple or vanilla
   extract
1 medium, tart apple, peeled,
   cored, and finely diced
$^1/_2$ cup raisins

1 cup rolled oats
$^3/_4$ cup plus 2 tablespoons all-
   purpose flour
$^1/_2$ cup whole wheat pastry flour
$^1/_2$ teaspoon salt
2 teaspoons baking powder
$^1/_2$ teaspoon baking soda
2 teaspoons cinnamon
For topping:
2 tablespoons granulated sugar
2 tablespoons chopped walnuts
$^1/_2$ teaspoon cinnamon

Preheat oven to 350°. Coat muffin cups with cooking spray. In large bowl, combine first 9 ingredients. Beat well with wooden spoon, then stir in oats. Set strainer over same bowl. Into it, measure flours, salt, baking powder, baking soda and cinnamon. With back of spoon, stir/sift contents onto batter below. Stir just to blend. Divide batter between muffin cups. Sprinkle on topping. Bake 22-25 minutes until risen, crisp and cake tester comes out dry. Cool a few minutes in pan, then lift out and cool on wire rack.
Yield: 12 2$^1/_2$" muffins

Susan G. Purdy
Roxbury

"I dream of the pastatime"

pasta and grain dishes to energize
Appalachian Trail hikers, Litchfield County
road runners, Pratt Center bird watchers
and Goshen Fair lumberjacks.

Pasta with Fresh Tomato Sauce

The better the ingredients, the better this dish will be. It's wonderful made with native Connecticut tomatoes and organic basil from Mrs. Collins' 7C Herb Farm on Baldwin Hill in New Preston.

2 large ripe tomatoes, diced
3 medium cloves garlic, minced
10 large basil leaves, torn into
   small pieces

6 tablespoons fruity olive oil
1 pound farfalle or other dry pasta
Parmigiano cheese

Combine all ingredients. Let sit 1 hour or refrigerate up to 8 hours. When ready to serve, bring sauce to room temperature. Cook pasta, toss sauce with hot pasta and top with freshly grated Parmigiano.
4 Servings

Adam Riess, Doc's
New Preston

Apricot Almond Rice Pilaf

This is especially pretty served in a glass dish. The fruits look like jewels surrounded by the golden rice.

$1^1/_2$ cups converted rice
2 tablespoons margarine
1 stalk celery, minced
1 medium onion, minced
$^1/_2$ teaspoon turmeric
$^1/_2$ cup dried apricots, slivered

$^1/_2$ cup golden raisins
Chicken broth
$^1/_4$ cup slivered almonds
1 cup fresh curly parsley, minced
Salt to taste

Rinse rice, set aside. Melt margarine in large saucepan. Sauté celery and onion until slightly cooked. Add turmeric. Add rice and mix, coating rice with margarine. Add apricots and raisins. Heat chicken broth; add to rice mixture to cover plus 1". Bring to boil; immediately turn down heat as low as possible. Cover and steam 45 minutes or until rice is cooked. Fluff with fork. Just before serving, add minced parsley, slivered almonds and salt.
6 Servings

Agnes Fairclough, East Coast Taco
New Milford

Linguine with Anchovy Mushroom Sauce

Anchovies give a wonderful depth to the flavor. Keep them a secret ingredient if necessary!

1 bunch scallions, white to light
   green part, chopped
1 large onion, sliced thin
$^1/_2$ cup olive oil, divided
12 ounces fresh mushrooms,
   sliced
1 clove garlic, minced

2 tablespoons finely chopped
   Italian parsley
2 tablespoons pine nuts
1 can anchovies, smashed to purée
1 pound linguine
1 stick butter
Parmesan cheese, freshly grated

Sauté scallions and onions in $^1/_4$ cup oil until soft, but not brown. Remove from pan. To the same pan, add mushrooms, garlic and parsley. Sauté until mushrooms are just cooked through. Add $^1/_4$ cup olive oil, pine nuts, anchovies and reserved onion mixture. Cook just until flavors blend. Cook pasta al dente. If sauce is too dry, add a bit of the pasta water before draining. Put half the butter in serving dish, add pasta, stir in remaining butter. Reserving some to garnish individual servings, mix balance of mushroom mixture into pasta. Sprinkle with grated cheese and reserved mushroom mixture.
6 Servings

Mary Cortina
New Milford

Noodle Pudding

This is a Lieberman family recipe and one of the Senator's favorites.

$^1/_2$ pound fine egg noodles
4 eggs
$^1/_2$ cup sugar
$1^3/_4$ cups cold water

Juice of 1 lemon
$^1/_4$ cup raisins, light or dark
1 teaspoon salt
1 teaspoon vanilla

Boil noodles until soft, drain thoroughly. Beat eggs until frothy. Combine remaining ingredients, mix well. Pour into ungreased 9"x13" glass baking pan; place in cold oven. Turn oven to 350°, bake for 1 hour.
6 Servings

Joseph I. Lieberman, U.S. Senator
Hartford

Penne Arrabbiato Primavera

I was introduced to this dish, also called "Angry Pasta" for its spiciness, in Positano, Italy. Members of the Chandon family (who also serve great Champagne) wrote the recipe out on a cloth napkin and each guest added a comment. The framed napkin hangs in my kitchen as a reminder of friends, good food and fun times.

$1/2$-$3/4$ cup virgin olive oil
3-5 cloves garlic, chopped
1 tablespoon red pepper flakes
3 broccoli florets, chopped
$1/8$ teaspoon fennel seeds
$1/4$ cup red wine
2 baby eggplant, sliced
$1/2$ pound porta fino or oyster
  mushrooms
1 tablespoon each, fresh rosemary,
  oregano and sage

$1/4$ cup fresh basil
1 28-ounce can imported plum
  tomatoes or 3-4 very ripe
  tomatoes
$1/4$ cup chopped parsley
1 pound imported penne or other
  pasta
$1/2$ cup freshly grated Parmigiano
  cheese
Basil leaves

Open a great bottle of wine. Heat olive oil in sauté pan and cook garlic. When brown, add red pepper flakes (the longer you cook the hotter it gets; if you intend to cook awhile, open another bottle of wine). Add broccoli, fennel and splash of red wine. Cover and start heating large pot of water for pasta containing a bit of olive oil and a garlic clove. Uncover sauté pan and add eggplant, mushrooms and herbs. Re-cover pan. Cut tomatoes into large chunks and add to sauté pan. Cover and cook on high heat until oil starts to appear on surface, about 15-20 minutes. Stir and lower flame. Cook pasta. Just before pasta is done, stir parsley into sauce and remove from heat. Drain pasta and serve with sauce over top. Garnish with Parmigiano and basil leaves.
6 Servings

Dr. Conrad Loreto
Washington

Green and White Noodles with Sweet Peppers and Sausage

The colors of the Italian flag. Light enough for lunch and at its absolute best made with fresh garden vegetables.

$1/2$ pound mild breakfast
    sausages, cut in $1/2$" pieces
$1/4$ cup water
$1/4$ cup olive oil
3 tablespoons finely chopped
    onion
3 ripe tomatoes, peeled, seeded
    and chopped

Salt and pepper
3 large sweet red peppers, cored,
    seeded and cut in 1" pieces
2 cups egg noodles
2 cups green noodles
2 tablespoons butter
$2/3$ cup grated Parmesan cheese

Cook sausage in water in large skillet until water has evaporated and sausage is browned; remove to bowl. Drain fat from skillet and add olive oil. Sauté onion until soft but not brown. Add tomatoes, salt, pepper and red peppers. Simmer, stirring until soft about 6 minutes. While sauce simmers, cook noodles, drain, put in warm bowl or platter. Pour sauce over and add butter. Toss. Add half the Parmesan cheese. Toss again. Top with remaining cheese.
6 Servings

Pamela Collins
New Milford

Creamy Baked Fusilli

This is a terrific dish with ham. It can be made ahead and baked at the last minute.

2 cups large curd cottage cheese
2 cups sour cream
$2/3$ cup finely chopped onions or
    scallions
2 large cloves garlic, minced
2 teaspoons Worcestershire sauce
8 drops Tabasco

2-4 tablespoons flour
$1/2$ teaspoon salt
$1/4$ teaspoon pepper
8 ounces cooked fusilli or other
    pasta twists
Buttered breadcrumbs for topping

Preheat oven to 350°. Mix first 6 ingredients together. Blend in flour, salt and pepper. Mix with cooked pasta. Turn into buttered casserole and sprinkle breadcrumbs on top. Bake 15 minutes until heated through and crumbs are brown.
8 Servings

Mimi Bender
Washington Depot

Emerald Rice

The perfect side dish. It works with meat, fish or fowl.

2 cups cooked rice
6 ounces Cheddar cheese, grated
3 eggs, well beaten
$^1/_3$ cup olive oil or butter
Dash of garlic salt, optional

1 medium onion, grated
2 cups light cream
1 cup chopped parsley
Salt and pepper to taste

Preheat oven to 250°. Combine ingredients and place in $1^1/_2$ quart casserole. Set casserole in pan of hot water in oven. Bake 1 hour or until all liquid has been absorbed and rice is fairly dry.
4-6 Servings

Helen Marx
New Milford

Pasta with Tender Sweet Kale

Kale is the star of the garden in beta-carotene and calcium. It's so versatile we layer it into scalloped potatoes, tuck it into paella, chop it into tomato sauce or soup and often substitute it for spinach. A favorite variety is Vates Dwarf Blue Curled Scotch which makes a pretty garden border and is tender and sweet all summer.

1 tablespoon olive oil
1 large onion, chopped
$^1/_2$ pound fresh mushrooms,
    sliced
2-3 cloves garlic, minced
8 cups fresh kale, torn from ribs

6 sundried tomatoes, sliced
1 cup French sorrel, chopped
1 pound pasta
3 tablespoons yoghurt
3 tablespoons freshly grated
    Parmesan

In large skillet, sauté onion in oil until soft. Add mushrooms and garlic; sauté 5 minutes. Stir in kale, tomatoes and sorrel. Cover tightly, steam until softened, about 10 minutes. Cook pasta. Toss pasta with kale mixture, yoghurt and Parmesan.
4-6 Servings

Diana Bristol, Bloomingfields Farm
Sherman

Grilled Basil Tomato Pizza

We love this pizza because it reminds us of our garden. Everyone is surprised when we cook it on the barbecue grill. Another delicious topping is smoked salmon, capers, sliced red onions and shredded Fontina cheese.

1 envelope active dry yeast	For topping (per pizza):
Pinch of sugar	$^1/_4$ cup grated Parmesan
1 cup warm water	6 slices fresh tomato
2$^1/_4$ teaspoons kosher salt	2 tablespoons chopped fresh basil
$^1/_4$ cup white cornmeal	2 cloves thinly sliced garlic
3 tablespoons whole wheat flour	Olive oil
1 tablespoon virgin olive oil	Salt and freshly ground pepper
2-3 cups unbleached white flour	

Dissolve sugar and yeast in warm water. After 5 minutes, stir in salt, cornmeal, wheat flour and oil. Gradually add 2 cups white flour, stirring with wooden spoon. Add third cup of flour as needed to make stiff dough. Knead dough on floured board for several minutes, until smooth. Put dough in bowl which has been brushed with olive oil. Coat dough with oil. Cover bowl with plastic wrap and let dough rise until double in bulk. Punch down and knead once more. Let dough rise again for about 40 minutes. Punch down. Cut into 4 pieces and wrap individually in plastic wrap. Refrigerate until needed, up to 3 days. (Do not freeze.) When ready to cook, prepare hot charcoal fire. On large oiled, inverted cookie sheet, spread and flatten dough into 12" oval. When fire is ready, push charcoal to one side so there is room for a brick or stone on part of grill. (You need a cooler area to put on toppings.) Lift dough carefully from baking sheet and put on grill over charcoal area. When pizza begins to bubble, move to cool area. Sprinkle with Parmesan and other topping ingredients. Slide pizza back to charcoal area and cook until grill marks appear on underside.
Yield: Four 12" pizzas

Kari and Hans Bauer
Litchfield

Mostaccioli with Broccoli Basil Sauce

This adaptable dish works as a first course, a side dish or an entrée in any season.

1 large bunch broccoli, about 1³/₄ pounds
¹/₂ cup olive oil
1¹/₂ tablespoons crushed garlic
1 cup chicken broth
¹/₄ cup chopped fresh basil

¹/₂ teaspoon dried oregano
Salt and pepper
9-12 ounces mostaccioli or other fresh pasta
¹/₂ cup freshly grated Parmesan cheese

Remove woody stems and stalks from broccoli and discard. Steam florets until crisp/tender, 5 minutes. Drain and plunge into ice water. When cool, drain and cut into 1/4" pieces. In medium saucepan, heat olive oil and sauté garlic until pale gold. Add chicken broth, basil, oregano, salt and pepper. Cook pasta. Just before done, add broccoli to sauce, heat through. Toss pasta with sauce and Parmesan cheese.
6 Servings

Frank Domanic
New Milford

Cheesy Noodles Florentine

This is great with grilled, butterflied leg of lamb or London broil. Add a salad, crusty bread and a Merlot or Pinot Noir. The recipe can be doubled.

¹/₃ cup creamy cottage cheese
2 ounces cream cheese
¹/₄ cup sour cream
1 package frozen chopped spinach, cooked and drained
¹/₄ cup white wine
6 scallions, chopped
1 teaspoon salt

¹/₂ teaspoon pepper
¹/₂ teaspoon freshly ground nutmeg
8 ounces medium width noodles
2 tablespoons grated Parmesan cheese
2 tablespoons butter

Preheat oven to 350°. Mix cottage cheese, cream cheese, sour cream, spinach and wine until smooth. Add scallions, salt, pepper and nutmeg. Stir well. Cook noodles. Drain. Butter 8 cup casserole well, add noodles. Pour spinach-cheese mixture over noodles, mix well. Sprinkle Parmesan cheese over noodles, dot with butter. Bake 30 minutes. Serve hot.
4 Servings

George Grizzard
New Preston

Basil Walnut Pesto for Pasta

We make this at summer's end with the basil harvest from our backyard garden. Since it freezes beautifully, we enjoy great, close-to-fresh basil flavor throughout the year. Double the recipe; use half and freeze half.

4 cups fresh basil leaves, divided
4 cloves garlic
1 teaspoon salt
$^{1}/_{2}$-1 cup chopped walnuts

1 cup olive oil
1 cup grated Parmesan or Romano
   cheese

Put one half the leaves and all other ingredients in food processor and whirl until chopped small and smooth. Add remaining basil and whirl again until smooth. Add more salt and garlic to taste.
Yield: 2 cups

Alan and Jean Chapin
New Preston

Fernhouse Pasta with No-Cook Creamy Sauce

Light, easy and low in fat, this dish suits our lifestyle in these hills. We serve it summer or winter with Fernhouse Salad.

$^{1}/_{2}$ cup no-fat sour cream
$^{1}/_{2}$ cup skim milk
1 scallion, finely sliced
$^{1}/_{4}$ cup fresh dill, minced

Pepper to taste
4 ounces rotini, radiatore or other
   small pasta

Mix together sour cream and milk until smooth and creamy. Add remaining ingredients. Refrigerate 2 hours or more to allow flavors to develop. Bring to room temperature before serving. Toss with hot pasta. Let stand a few minutes, then toss again.
2 Servings

Patricia and Kermit Adler
New Milford

Doc's Pizza

For the best results in a home oven, bake this pizza on preheated terra-cotta tiles.

For dough:
1¹/₂ cups warm water
4 teaspoons dry yeast
¹/₂ cup extra virgin olive oil
¹/₂ cup fine ground cornmeal
4¹/₄ cups bread flour
¹/₂ tablespoon salt
¹/₂ cup all-purpose flour
¹/₂ cup coarse ground cornmeal
For toppings:
Finnochio - roasted fennel, roasted garlic, tomato sauce and fresh mozzarella

Sparrow - Ricotta, fresh mozzarella, cooked asparagus and fresh tomato
Marinara - tomato sauce, garlic, crushed red pepper, capers, anchovies, mozzarella and oregano
Margherta - fresh mozzarella, sliced tomato and fresh basil
For finishing:
Olive oil
Salt and pepper

Put warm water in bowl of electric mixer and sprinkle yeast on surface. Let sit 10 minutes. Stir briefly. Let sit 5 minutes. Stir in olive oil. Add fine cornmeal, bread flour, and salt; mix with dough hook at medium speed 5 minutes. Knead dough briefly by hand, then place in lightly oiled bowl. Cover tightly with plastic wrap. Let rise 1¹/₂ hours until doubled in size. Punch down and let rise until doubled again, about 1¹/₂ hours. Preheat oven and tiles to 500°. Divide dough into quarters. As needed, sprinkle work surface with all purpose flour and roll out four 9" rounds. Sprinkle a pizza peel or back of cookie sheet with coarse cornmeal. Place dough on top and add toppings. Finish with sprinkle of olive oil and salt and pepper to taste. Slide pizza off peel or sheet onto tiles and bake 7 minutes or until golden brown.
Yield: 4 pizzas

**Adam Riess, Doc's
New Preston**

Evergreen Farm Summer Pasta

This recipe embraces the bounty of summer. Give your guests a basket and glass of wine and invite them to gather the ingredients. Compost the trimmings.

2 dozen ripe, medium tomatoes
Olive oil
Fresh basil, chopped
Freshly ground pepper
Assorted fresh garden vegetables,
    chopped

Fresh garden herbs
Fresh pasta
Locatelli cheese, coarsely grated

Make tomato sauce: heat oil in large, heavy saucepan. Wash and quarter tomatoes, add to oil. Cook gently a few hours, stirring frequently. Cool sauce. Put sauce through Vev-Inox (an Italian tomato processor) or food mill. Return to pan. Add generous amounts of fresh basil and ground pepper. Simmer slowly, reducing to desired thickness. Add vegetables according to cooking time required; i.e., limas, string beans, peppers, carrots, leeks, kohlrabi and onions first, then eggplant (after salting, standing and draining for 30 minutes), then broccoli, Swiss chard and squashes. Add fresh herbs such as oregano, chervil, thyme, tarragon, sage or chives. Cook until vegetables are tender but firm. Serve on pasta, topped with cheese.

Susan Payne, Evergreen Farm
Washington

Very Veggie Tabooli Salad

Bulgur #2 is similar to wheat germ and is available at health food stores.

$^3/_4$ cup bulgur wheat #2
Water to cover
1 bunch romaine lettuce
1 bunch Italian parsley
2 bunches scallions
1 medium-large onion
4 plum tomatoes

$^1/_4$ cup dried mint, crushed
$^1/_4$ teaspoon allspice
$^1/_8$-$^1/_4$ cup olive oil
Juice of 2-3 lemons
Salt and pepper
Pita bread

Soak bulgur wheat in water 15 minutes. Drain. Chop all vegetables finely. Add drained bulgur. Sprinkle with mint and allspice. Toss all with olive oil and lemon juice. Salt and pepper to taste. Serve with pita bread.
4-6 Servings

Christine Tyson
New Milford

Indian Style Basmati Rice

Serve with Indian Style Chicken in Spiced Coconut Milk.

4 cups chicken stock
2 cups basmati rice
3 large potatoes, cut in $^1/_2$" cubes
1 teaspoon salt
$^1/_3$ cup butter
1 carrot, scraped and finely chopped
3 large cloves garlic, minced
1 teaspoon turmeric

$^1/_4$ teaspoon ground cloves
Pinch cinnamon
2 tablespoons grated fresh ginger
$^1/_4$ cup chopped fresh cilantro
$^1/_2$ teaspoon cayenne
$^1/_2$ cup vegetable oil
1 large red Bermuda onion, julienned

In heavy saucepan, bring stock and rice to boil. Cover and cook until rice is tender and fluffy, 15-20 minutes. In another saucepan, place potatoes and salt and barely cover with cold water. Bring to boil and lower to simmer, cooking until potatoes are fork tender, 8 minutes. Remove from heat and drain. In large skillet, heat butter over medium heat. Add potatoes and sauté until soft. Add remaining ingredients except oil and onion, stirring until blended. Remove from heat and stir into cooked rice. Meanwhile, heat vegetable oil in skillet over medium high heat. Sauté onion until cooked and deep brown, 8-10 minutes. Drain onions and use to garnish rice.
8 Servings

Liba H. Furhman
New Milford

Angel Hair Pasta with Shrimp and Champagne

1 cup sliced mushrooms
1 tablespoon olive oil
1 pound medium shrimp, shelled
$1^1/_2$ cups Champagne
$^1/_4$ teaspoon salt

2 tablespoons minced shallots or scallions
2 plum tomatoes, diced
1 cup heavy cream, divided
1 pound angel hair pasta
3 tablespoons chopped parsley

Sauté mushrooms in medium saucepan in hot olive oil. Cook just long enough to release and evaporate mushroom juices. Remove mushrooms, set aside. In same saucepan, combine shrimp, Champagne and salt. Over high heat, bring to simmer. When liquid just boils, shrimp are done. Remove shrimp, set aside. Add shallots and tomatoes to cooking liquid. Boil until liquid is reduced to $^1/_2$ cup (about 8 minutes). Then add $^3/_4$ cup heavy cream and boil 1-2 minutes until slightly thickened and reduced. Add shrimp and mushrooms to sauce; heat through. Season to taste. Cook and drain pasta, return to pot. Toss with remaining $^1/_4$ cup cream and parsley. Spoon shrimp and sauce over pasta.
4 Servings

Suzanne H. Gallup
New Milford

Peg's Peanut Butter Chicken Over Pasta

I first tasted this at a dinner party at my friend Peg's. Children love it as much as adults. It travels well and is especially good on hot, humid nights.

2 13³/₄-ounce cans low-salt
   chicken broth
4 peppercorns
Sprinkle of dried celery flakes
Sprinkle of dried onion flakes
6 bay leaves
4-5 boneless chicken breasts
¹/₂ cup peanut butter
2 tablespoons minced fresh ginger
¹/₄ cup sweet, thick soy sauce
6 tablespoons sesame oil, divided

2 tablespoons fresh garlic, minced
2 tablespoons red wine vinegar
2 teaspoons Tabasco
¹/₂ cup heavy cream
2 tablespoons sugar, optional
1 pound spaghetti or other thin
   pasta
1 small cucumber, thinly sliced
1 can water chestnuts, drained
   and thinly sliced
1 can Oriental baby ears of corn

Add peppercorns, celery flakes, onion flakes and bay leaves to broth. Heat to simmer. Add chicken; poach 10 minutes. Remove chicken to cool, saving broth. Reduce broth by half. Cool and strain. In food processor, combine peanut butter, ginger, soy sauce, 4 tablespoons sesame oil, garlic and vinegar. With motor running, add ³/₄ cup broth, Tabasco and heavy cream. Sauce should be thick but pourable; add more broth if necessary. Add sugar if desired. Cook and drain pasta, toss with remaining 2 tablespoons sesame oil. Shred chicken into bite-sized pieces. Place pasta on platter, then chicken, then sauce. Garnish with cucumber, water chestnuts and corn.
4-6 Servings

Carol Harris
New Milford

Deb's Quick Bolognese Sauce

Your guests will think you slaved for hours and it simmered for days! This sauce is even better made a day ahead, but don't add the cream until just before serving.

2 tablespoons butter
¹/₂ medium fennel bulb, coarsely
    chopped
1 small onion, chopped fine
1 carrot, chopped fine
³/₄ pound lean ground beef
¹/₂ cup dry red wine

1 16-ounce can crushed tomatoes
    in purée
¹/₄ cup heavy cream
Salt and freshly ground pepper
1 pound pasta, cooked
Parmesan cheese

In large saucepan, heat butter until melted, add chopped vegetables. Sauté until soft, 5-10 minutes. Add beef and cook, breaking into small pieces, over medium low heat until it loses its pink color. Add wine, simmer until alcohol evaporates, 2 minutes. Add tomatoes, bring to boil. Partially cover, reduce heat and simmer until sauce thickens, 20 minutes. Stir in heavy cream. Do not boil! Add salt and pepper to taste. To serve, pour sauce over pasta and garnish with cheese.
4 Servings

Deborah Slatcher
New Milford

Fresh Linguine with Ratatouille Sauce

This recipe takes advantage of almost all the vegetables in your summer garden.

¹/₂ cup chopped onion
2 garlic cloves, minced
1 tablespoon olive oil
4 medium ripe tomatoes, chopped
1¹/₂ cups eggplant, peeled and cubed
1 cup zucchini, sliced
¹/₂ cup chopped green pepper
1 8-ounce can tomato sauce
2 tablespoons chopped fresh parsley

1 tablespoon chopped fresh oregano
1 tablespoon chopped fresh basil
¹/₄ teaspoon sugar
¹/₄ teaspoon salt
¹/₈ teaspoon pepper
4 teaspoons cornstarch
1 tablespoon water
Parmesan cheese, freshly grated
9 ounces fresh linguine, cooked

Cook onion and garlic in hot oil until tender, but not brown. Stir in next 11 ingredients. Bring to boil. Reduce heat. Cover and simmer mixture 15-20 minutes, stirring occasionally. Mix together cornstarch and water. Add to tomato mixture. Stir, cook mixture until thick and bubbly, 3-4 minutes. Serve over pasta. Top with Parmesan cheese.
4 Servings

Vicky Sussman
Washington Depot

Orange Rice with Mint

A rich, but refreshing taste. Delicious any season.

1^1/$_2$ cups white rice
^{1}/$_2$ cup finely chopped onion
4 tablespoons butter
4 tablespoons grated orange rind
Salt and pepper

3 cups chicken broth
^{3}/$_4$ cup orange juice
1 tablespoon chopped fresh mint
^{1}/$_2$ cup pine nuts

Preheat oven to 325°. Sauté chopped onion in butter until soft. Stir in raw rice. Add orange rind, salt and freshly ground pepper. Combine with chicken broth, orange juice and mint in ovenproof casserole. Bake rice, uncovered, 1 hour. Add a little broth or water if rice becomes too dry. In last 10 minutes, mix in pine nuts. If, in 1 hour, rice is not done, turn oven up to 375°, cover casserole loosely with foil, and cook an additional 5-10 minutes. 4 Servings

Kathryn Popper
South Kent

Fowl play

poultry takes off in innovative entrées
for homecoming hot air ballooners,
scenic railroad riders,
cherished weekend guests.

Roast Chicken with Fennel

This dish is best if you can refrigerate the chicken spread with the garlic rosemary paste for 24 hours before roasting.

1 whole 3¹/₂ pound free-range or organic chicken
2 tablespoons extra virgin olive oil
Freshly ground black pepper
3 large garlic cloves, crushed
1¹/₂ tablespoons minced fresh rosemary

2 medium or 1 large fennel bulb
1 large yellow onion
¹/₂ cup dry white wine
¹/₂ cup "hot links" sausage, chopped
¹/₄ teaspoon salt

Wash and dry chicken, removing excess fat, reserving giblets. Cover with olive oil and black pepper. Using fork or mortar and pestle, mix garlic with rosemary to make paste. Spread mixture over chicken and place in 9"x13" glass baking dish. Preheat oven to 450°. Remove grassy top from fennel bulb; mince leaves finely, julienne the stems, and cut bulb lengthwise into ¹/₄" slices. Peel onion and cut into eighths lengthwise. Surround bird with sliced fennel bulb and onions. Bake 30 minutes. Reduce heat to 350° and pour wine over chicken. Scatter giblets, sausage and julienned fennel stems around chicken. Sprinkle chicken with salt. Return dish to oven. Baste every 15 minutes. Cook 45 minutes more, or until juices run clear. Remove from oven, sprinkle with minced green fennel top, let rest for 10 minutes.
4 Servings

Michael Chelminski
Bridgewater

Sour Cream Stuffed Chicken with New Potatoes

Make this a complete dinner by adding a fresh garden salad and white wine or Champagne.

1 roasting chicken
¹/₂ lemon
Salt and freshly ground pepper
Fresh sage or basil, chopped
1 cup sour cream

1 teaspoon Dijon mustard
Sweet butter
Sesame oil
New potatoes

Preheat oven to 350°. Rub whole cleaned chicken with lemon, salt and pepper. Mix together 1 tablespoon chopped sage or basil, sour cream and mustard. Stuff chicken with mixture and close with toothpicks. Roast chicken 1 to 1¹/₂ hours, basting with mix of melted butter and sesame oil. About 45 minutes before chicken is done, add new potatoes coating them with pan juices. Sprinkle them with additional chopped sage or basil.

Diane von Furstenberg
New Milford

Bourbon Street Chicken

A Villager favorite! Nice served with wild rice pilaf.

2 large boneless, skinless chicken
    breast halves
$^1/_2$ cup all-purpose flour
Powdered Cajun spice mix to taste
2-3 tablespoons olive oil

$^1/_2$ cup white wine or chicken broth
1 tablespoon fresh tarragon,
    chopped
$^1/_4$ cup heavy cream
$^1/_2$ teaspoon Dijon mustard

Pound chicken breasts to $^1/_4$" thickness, between sheets of waxed paper. Preheat 10-12" skillet over medium high heat. Combine flour and Cajun spice and rub into both sides of chicken. Add oil to skillet, heat to near smoking point and add chicken breasts. Cook 3 minutes per side or until firm, juices just running clear. Remove to warm plate. Add wine or stock to skillet, scraping up brown bits and cook until reduced by half. Add tarragon and cream and reduce until almost thick. Stir in mustard; pour sauce over chicken and serve.
2 Servings

Bill Leo, The Villager Restaurant
Kent

Stir Fried Chicken Strips with Vegetables

Though this is good any season, it's at its best with fresh local vegetables and home grown basil. It's fast, tasty, and kindly to those watching their cholesterol. Try it with turkey, too.

$^1/_4$ cup chicken broth
$^1/_4$ cup white wine Worcestershire
    sauce
$^1/_2$ teaspoon cornstarch
$^1/_2$ teaspoon dried basil, crushed
$^1/_2$ teaspoon garlic, minced
$^1/_4$ teaspoon onion powder
Dash cayenne pepper

2 tablespoons margarine
2 boneless, skinless chicken breast
    halves
$1^1/_2$ cups mixed fresh broccoli,
    baby carrots, red peppers and
    water chestnuts
Chow mein or rice noodles

Stir together chicken broth, Worcestershire sauce, cornstarch, basil, garlic, onion powder and cayenne; set aside. Rinse chicken and pat dry. Cut chicken into $^1/_2$" strips. In medium skillet, melt margarine. Sauté chicken over medium heat for 2-3 minutes, turning occasionally. Add vegetables. Cook while stirring, about 2 minutes more. Add chicken broth mixture, stirring as you pour it in. Continue stirring until thickened and bubbly, about 2 minutes more. Serve over noodles.
2 Servings

Sydell Brenner, Northville Supermarket
New Milford

Biscuit Topped Chicken Pot Pie

A dish much requested by guests for summer dinners and winter lunches. Free range chickens are best, and red currant jelly is the perfect condiment.

For chicken:
1 chicken, quartered
Water to cover
1 stick butter
2 large onions, peeled
2 carrots
2 celery stalks
4 sprigs parsley
1 tablespoon tarragon
2 teaspoons salt
$^1/_4$ teaspoon freshly ground
    pepper
For vegetables:
1 cup peas
3 large carrots, peeled and sliced

24 pearl onions, peeled
Reserved chicken broth
For sauce:
$^1/_4$ cup butter
$^1/_4$ cup flour
Reserved chicken broth
$^1/_4$ teaspoon Tabasco
Salt and pepper to taste
For biscuits:
2 cups sifted flour
1 tablespoon baking powder
$^1/_2$ teaspoon salt
$^1/_4$ cup shortening or butter
$^3/_4$ cup milk
1 tablespoon sugar

Place chicken in large pot. Add water just to cover and bring to boil. Skim foam. Add remaining ingredients, reduce to simmer. Cover. Simmer 1 hour. Uncover and let cool 4 hours in refrigerator. Skim fat. Strain broth and put back into pot. Set aside chicken, discard vegetables. Pick meat from chicken and reserve. Place uncooked vegetables in cheesecloth, tie with string. Boil in chicken broth 15 minutes. Remove. In 14" oval au gratin dish, put layer of chicken pieces, then layer of vegetables, alternating until all are used. Skim fat from chicken broth. Melt butter. Add flour and whisk until smooth. Add mixture to chicken broth. Add Tabasco, salt and pepper. Simmer 5 minutes. Slowly pour over chicken and vegetables. Preheat oven to 450°. Make biscuits. Sift flour, baking powder, salt and sugar into bowl. Cut in shortening. Add milk and stir quickly until dough clings together. Turn out on floured board, knead a few times, and pat or roll out to $^1/_4$"-$^1/_2$" thickness. Cut into 2" rounds with floured cutter. Place on top of pie. Bake 12-15 minutes until light brown.
6 Servings

Bill Blass
New Preston

Mother's Southern Fried Chicken

I prepared this dish as a two-time guest chef at the former Mary Dugan's in New Milford. My mother, who was born and raised in Missouri, taught me how to make it. It's great the next day, so it's easy to prepare ahead for a picnic.

2-3 best quality fryers, cut up
1¹/₂ cups flour
2 teaspoons salt
2 teaspoons pepper
Parsley

Garlic
Cajun spices
Oregano
1-2 cups canned Crisco

Double up two lunch bag sized paper bags. Put flour, salt and pepper, and other spices to your taste in doubled bag. Shake to mix. In the meantime, melt enough Crisco over medium to medium high heat to fill 12" skillet half full. Place two pieces of chicken at a time in bag with flour mixture and shake until well coated. Drop into heated melted shortening and cook, uncovered, approximately 15 minutes per side or until crispy brown. Try to handle chicken as little as possible while cooking. As pieces are done, put them on flat pan lined with paper towels to drain. Keep warm in 200° oven while rest of chicken fries.
6 Servings

Marty Sweeney
Dover Plains, NY

Hot Chicken Salad Casserole

This dish was created when friends dropped in to visit during a fall foliage tour. It's very fast and the ingredients are often already on hand.

2 cups cooked chicken, coarsely
    chopped
2 cups thinly sliced celery
¹/₂ cup blanched, salted, chopped
    almonds
¹/₃ cup chopped green pepper
2 tablespoons chopped pimento

2 tablespoons minced onion
¹/₂ teaspoon salt
2 tablespoons lemon juice
¹/₂ cup mayonnaise, preferably
    homemade
3 cups crushed potato chips

Preheat oven to 350°. Combine all ingredients except chips. Turn into greased 1¹/₂ quart casserole. Sprinkle with crushed chips. Bake 25 minutes.
3-4 Servings

Murry Morgenstern
New Milford

Doc's Pizza

For the best results in a home oven, bake this pizza on preheated terracotta tiles.

For dough:
1 1/2 cups warm water
4 teaspoons dry yeast
1/2 cup extra virgin olive oil
1/2 cup fine ground cornmeal
4 1/4 cups bread flour
1/2 tablespoon salt
1/2 cup all-purpose flour
1/2 cup coarse ground cornmeal
For toppings:
Finnochio - roasted fennel, roasted garlic, tomato sauce and fresh mozzarella

Sparrow - Ricotta, fresh mozzarella, cooked asparagus and fresh tomato
Marinara - tomato sauce, garlic, crushed red pepper, capers, anchovies, mozzarella and oregano
Margherta - fresh mozzarella, sliced tomato and fresh basil
For finishing:
Olive oil
Salt and pepper

Put warm water in bowl of electric mixer and sprinkle yeast on surface. Let sit 10 minutes. Stir briefly. Let sit 5 minutes. Stir in olive oil. Add fine cornmeal, bread flour, and salt; mix with dough hook at medium speed 5 minutes. Knead dough briefly by hand, then place in lightly oiled bowl. Cover tightly with plastic wrap. Let rise 1 1/2 hours until doubled in size. Punch down and let rise until doubled again, about 1 1/2 hours. Preheat oven and tiles to 500°. Divide dough into quarters. As needed, sprinkle work surface with all purpose flour and roll out four 9" rounds. Sprinkle a pizza peel or back of cookie sheet with coarse cornmeal. Place dough on top and add toppings. Finish with sprinkle of olive oil and salt and pepper to taste. Slide pizza off peel or sheet onto tiles and bake 7 minutes or until golden brown.
Yield: 4 pizzas

Adam Riess, Doc's
New Preston

Deb's Quick Bolognese Sauce

Your guests will think you slaved for hours and it simmered for days! This sauce is even better made a day ahead, but don't add the cream until just before serving.

2 tablespoons butter
$^1/_2$ medium fennel bulb, coarsely
   chopped
1 small onion, chopped fine
1 carrot, chopped fine
$^3/_4$ pound lean ground beef
$^1/_2$ cup dry red wine

1 16-ounce can crushed tomatoes
   in purée
$^1/_4$ cup heavy cream
Salt and freshly ground pepper
1 pound pasta, cooked
Parmesan cheese

In large saucepan, heat butter until melted, add chopped vegetables. Sauté until soft, 5-10 minutes. Add beef and cook, breaking into small pieces, over medium low heat until it loses its pink color. Add wine, simmer until alcohol evaporates, 2 minutes. Add tomatoes, bring to boil. Partially cover, reduce heat and simmer until sauce thickens, 20 minutes. Stir in heavy cream. Do not boil! Add salt and pepper to taste. To serve, pour sauce over pasta and garnish with cheese.
4 Servings

Deborah Slatcher
New Milford

Fresh Linguine with Ratatouille Sauce

This recipe takes advantage of almost all the vegetables in your summer garden.

$^1/_2$ cup chopped onion
2 garlic cloves, minced
1 tablespoon olive oil
4 medium ripe tomatoes, chopped
$1^1/_2$ cups eggplant, peeled and cubed
1 cup zucchini, sliced
$^1/_2$ cup chopped green pepper
1 8-ounce can tomato sauce
2 tablespoons chopped fresh parsley

1 tablespoon chopped fresh oregano
1 tablespoon chopped fresh basil
$^1/_4$ teaspoon sugar
$^1/_4$ teaspoon salt
$^1/_8$ teaspoon pepper
4 teaspoons cornstarch
1 tablespoon water
Parmesan cheese, freshly grated
9 ounces fresh linguine, cooked

Cook onion and garlic in hot oil until tender, but not brown. Stir in next 11 ingredients. Bring to boil. Reduce heat. Cover and simmer mixture 15-20 minutes, stirring occasionally. Mix together cornstarch and water. Add to tomato mixture. Stir, cook mixture until thick and bubbly, 3-4 minutes. Serve over pasta. Top with Parmesan cheese.
4 Servings

Vicky Sussman
Washington Depot

Roast Duckling with Fresh Raspberry Sauce

This dish is especially delicious made with our wonderful local raspberries.

1 5-6 pound duck for each 2
    guests
Soy sauce
Brown stock or good chicken
    bouillon, mixed with 1-2
    tablespoons tomato paste

For sauce:
1 cup chopped onions
$^1/_4$ cup vegetable oil
1 cup white wine
$^1/_2$ cup raspberry or cider vinegar
1 cup raspberries
Duck stock
4 tablespoons cornstarch

Preheat oven to 375°. Remove gizzards and necks from ducks and place them on bottom of roasting pan. Do not include livers. Cut off wings at second joint, cut off tails and excess neck skin and add these to roasting pan. With sharp fork, prick duck skin, trying not to pierce meat. Rub ducks with soy sauce and place them in roasting pan on top of wings and trimmings. Roast for 2-2$^1/_2$ hours until skin comes away from meat. Remove ducks from pan, let cool. Discard fat from pan, reserving juices. Make duck stock: put trimmings in saucepan. Add water to roasting pan and place on low burner. Scrape all juices from bottom and add to saucepan. Add stock to cover and simmer 1 hour. Make sauce: brown onions in oil until crisp. Add wine, vinegar and raspberries and reduce by $^1/_2$. Add duck stock and simmer until flavors are well blended. Strain sauce into another saucepan and bring to boil. Dissolve cornstarch with water and adjust thickness of sauce to coat back of spoon. When ready to serve, preheat oven to 475°. Split ducks in half and place skin side up in roasting pan. Place pan in oven and roast until skin is crisp, 30-45 minutes. Serve with sauce.

Maison Le Blanc
New Milford

Grilled Breast of Chicken with Date Relish and Fennel Fondue

6 8-ounce boneless chicken breasts
For date relish:
2 cups dates, cut into quarters
3 tablespoons fennel stalk, cut thin
　　on bias
2 tablespoons minced shallots
3 tablespoons chopped chives
3 tablespoons chopped cilantro

$^1/_2$ cup orange juice
1 cup olive oil
1 clove garlic, minced
Salt and cayenne pepper to taste
For fennel fondue:
3 fennel bulbs, cut into thin strips
2 cups water
2 ounces olive oil

Mix relish ingredients together and allow flavor to marry at least 2 hours. Cook fondue ingredients in stainless steel pan, covered, for $^1/_2$ hour. Grill chicken breasts over charcoal fire. To serve, place $^1/_2$ cup of fennel fondue on plate. Cut chicken breast twice on the bias, and fan out on top of fondue. Surround chicken with $^1/_2$ cup of relish.
6 Servings

The Mayflower Inn
Washington

Crunchy Parmesan Chicken

I have used this recipe for 25 years. It's my standby and it's fantastic. Prepare it ahead (it can be frozen without the potatoes) and pop it into the oven when guests arrive.

8 skinless, boneless chicken thighs
6 tablespoons butter
4 cloves garlic, minced
$^3/_4$ cup flavored bread crumbs

$^3/_4$ cup grated Parmesan cheese
Salt and pepper to taste
12 or more small red potatoes
　　(optional)

Preheat oven to 375°. Briefly sauté garlic in butter. Wash and trim thighs and pat dry. Mix crumbs and Parmesan in pie dish. Roll thighs in garlic butter, then in cheese/crumb mixture, reserving some of each mixture if using potatoes. Place thighs in ungreased 9"x13" baking dish, tucking edges so they appear to be rolled. Add potatoes if desired, sprinkling them with some of the crumb mixture. Drizzle remaining garlic butter over all. Bake 45 minutes.
4-6 Servings

Faith Ohms
Litchfield

Jewish American Princess Fried Chicken

1 fresh, cut-up fryer	Salt and pepper to taste
Vegetable oil	1 tablespoon paprika
Butter	1 tablespoon Cajun spice
1^1/$_2$ cups flour	

Send chauffeur to your favorite butcher shop for the chicken (save the brown paper bag). Have your cook 1) Melt equal parts oil and butter ^{3}/$_4$" deep in skillet over moderate heat. 2) Put flour, seasoned with remaining ingredients, into brown paper bag. 3) Rinse chicken parts and place in bag. Then you tightly close top of bag (watch your nails) and shake 10 times. Hand bag to Cook, go dress for dinner. While you dress, have Cook pre-heat oven to 350° and brown chicken slowly in skillet. When evenly browned, have Cook place chicken in dish in oven. Have Cook prepare rest of meal while you touch up your makeup. In about ^{1}/$_2$ hour, voilà! Dinner is served! You must be exhausted.
2 Servings

Whoopi Goldberg
Cornwall

Chicken with Mustard and Leek Sauce

This is easy, elegant and everyone likes it including my five-year-old. It's especially good with leeks from your garden. Serve with brown rice and sautéed carrots.

4 boneless, skinless chicken breast halves	1 tablespoon butter
^{1}/$_2$ cup flour	2 tablespoons Cognac or sherry
Salt and pepper	1 cup chicken broth
2 medium-sized leeks	^{1}/$_2$ cup half and half
2 tablespoons peanut oil	2 tablespoons minced gherkins
	1 tablespoon mustard

Pound chicken breasts to flatten. Season with salt and pepper. Dredge in flour and set aside. Trim off tough green leaves and root ends of leeks. Split lengthwise. Rinse well under running water to remove dirt; then dice. Heat oil and butter and sauté chicken on each side until golden. Remove chicken from pan or skillet. Using same pan, sauté leeks until wilted. Add Cognac and boil until almost evaporated. Add broth and simmer about 2 minutes. Add half and half, gherkins, mustard and pepper to taste. Bring to boil. Add chicken to pan, turning to coat with sauce. Cover and simmer until chicken is tender and cooked through.
4 Servings

Amelia M. Jimenez
Bridgewater

Chicken Breasts Stuffed with Shitakes, Sundried Tomatoes and Basil

This is the first dish I served at a Litchfield Hills dinner party. It's terrific for entertaining; you can stuff the chicken 4-6 hours ahead. Serve with herb-roasted red potatoes and a fresh squash and carrot sauté.

For basil purée:
2 bunches basil
$1/8$ cup olive oil
For basil sauce:
1 tablespoon olive oil
2 shallots, chopped
$1^1/2$ cups white wine
Basil stems
$1^1/2$ quarts chicken stock
$1/2$ cup heavy cream
4 tablespoons basil purée

For stuffing:
1 tablespoon olive oil
4 ounces shitake mushrooms,
    destemmed and thinly sliced
2 ounces sundried tomatoes in oil,
    julienned
1 ounce balsamic vinegar
2 tablespoons basil purée
1 tablespoon flour
Salt and pepper to taste
4 whole chicken breasts, skin on
    and bone in
Olive oil

To make basil purée: clean, dry and destem basil, saving stems. Put part of leaves in food processor and slowly add oil. Add remainder of leaves and purée. (There will be leftover purée. Store with thin layer of oil on top.) To make sauce: sauté shallots in olive oil until translucent. Add white wine and basil stems. Reduce by two-thirds. Add chicken stock, reduce by two-thirds. Add heavy cream, reduce by one-half. Strain. (Basil purée will be added to sauce right before serving.) To make stuffing: in medium sauté pan, over medium heat, add 1 tablespoon olive oil and sauté mushrooms until slightly limp. Add tomatoes and sauté 3 minutes more. Add vinegar (off heat, to prevent splattering). Cook 2 minutes. Add 2 tablespoons basil purée, stir well. Stir in flour to bind mixture. Season with salt and pepper. Remove from heat and let cool. Preheat oven to 400°. Loosen skin from meat with your fingers, stuff mixture under skin of chicken. Be sure to cover all meat with stuffing. Coat chicken skin with oil and season with salt and pepper. Place on cookie sheet, bone down. Cook 25-28 minutes. Remove from oven and let sit for 2-3 minutes. Remove bones. Now add purée to sauce and serve over chicken.
4 Servings

**Earl S. Mulley, ESM Catering
Sherman**

Chicken Pot Pie with Root Vegetables

Thé Café prepares this dish as individual pies; each toasty brown crust is decorated with a cut-out pastry chicken.

1 whole chicken, roasted
Potatoes, cut in 1" cubes
Sweet potatoes, cut in 1" cubes
Turnip, cut in 1" cubes
Carrots, cut in $1/4$" slices
Celery, cut in $1/4$" slices
Leeks, white and some green, cut in $1/4$" slices
Fresh pearl onions, peeled
Frozen peas, thawed

For sauce:
8 tablespoons sweet butter
11 tablespoons unbleached white flour
3 cups chicken stock
White pepper and salt to taste
For topping:
Your favorite pie crust dough
Egg wash

Remove skin and bones from chicken and cut into large chunks. Steam vegetables (except peas) or cook in chicken stock until just underdone. Prepare sauce. Heat butter in heavy saucepan; add flour, stirring constantly 2 minutes without letting roux brown. Continue cooking over low heat 10 minutes to cook flour. Heat stock in separate saucepan, add to flour and butter mixture, beating with wire whisk until smooth. Simmer gently 30 minutes, stirring frequently until sauce is thickened. Sauce consistency can be adjusted by adding stock or milk, or bits of a butter/flour mixture. Season with salt and pepper. Add chicken and enough vegetables to sauce to achieve desired density, remembering that vegetables will absorb some liquid in cooking. Stir in peas. Taste and season. Pour into casserole. Top with crust, ventilated with cuts to release steam. Brush with egg wash. Cook until crust is done and filling is hot and bubbly.
4-6 Servings

Toni Ripinsky and Chris Zaima, Thé Café
New Preston

Hunter's Chicken

An old family favorite that makes a great dinner party entrée. It's comforting, colorful and especially delicious when accompanied by fresh peas and baked polenta with Gorgonzola. Be ready to serve seconds.

$^1/_2$ cup extra virgin olive oil
14 skinless, boneless chicken
   breast halves
2 cups unbleached flour
1 large onion, finely diced
6 cloves garlic, finely minced
6 ounces sliced pancetta, chopped
5 tablespoons chopped fresh
   rosemary

1 pound mushrooms, quartered
   and sautéed
$2^1/_2$ cups dry Marsala
6 cups canned, whole Italian
   tomatoes including juice
Salt and freshly ground pepper to
   taste
Parsley or basil for garnish

Heat oil in large skillet. Dip each breast in flour shaking off excess. Brown breasts on both sides. Place breasts in large oven-proof dish in one layer. Reduce heat under skillet to medium. Add onion, garlic, pancetta, rosemary and mushrooms. Add Marsala, continue cooking and stirring until wine is almost all reduced. Break up tomatoes and add with juice to skillet. Bring sauce to boil for few minutes to reduce and thicken liquid. Reduce heat to medium, add salt and pepper, partially cover and let simmer 30 minutes. Pour sauce over browned chicken breasts, making sure they are completely covered. Cover lightly with foil and bake in 350° oven (do not preheat) for 1 hour, basting occasionally and uncovering for last 10 minutes. If too much juice forms at top, spoon off. Sprinkle with parsley or basil before serving.
10 + Servings

Karen Silk
Washington

Lincoln's Portable Pineapple Chicken

The chicken packets can be prepared ahead and then grilled at the beach or poolside. This is a delicious and infinitely expandable recipe.

1 chicken breast per person
Sliced mushrooms
Sliced onions
Chopped green pepper
Pineapple chunks with juice
For sauce:
Tarragon vinegar

Soy sauce
Melted butter
Oregano
Garlic powder
Salt and freshly ground pepper to
   taste.

Brown chicken in oven. Reset oven to 325°. Cut one large square of heavy duty foil for each breast. Place generous amount of vegetables on piece of foil, then some pineapple and juice. Combine sauce ingredients and pour small amount over vegetables. Place chicken breast on top of vegetables; add a little more sauce. Wrap each package, sealing ends securely. When ready to serve, grill (or bake) approximately 25 minutes.

Lynette Cornell
Washington Depot

Sweet and Spicy Chicken Breasts

An intriguing blend of ingredients gives this simple dish a complex flavor.

2 chicken breasts, halved and cut
   into serving size
$1/3$ cup flour
Salt and black pepper
2 tablespoons oil
1 onion, chopped
1 clove garlic, finely chopped
4 tomatoes, skinned and
   quartered

$1^1/_2$ cups dry white wine
$1/_2$ teaspoon thyme
$1/_2$ teaspoon oregano
$1/_2$ teaspoon crushed hot red
   pepper, or to taste
2 carrots, diced
1 cup pimento-stuffed olives
8 dried prunes

Rub chicken breasts with flour seasoned with salt and black pepper. Heat oil in heavy skillet and brown chicken breasts on both sides. Add onion and garlic and sauté until onion is tender. Add tomatoes, wine, thyme, oregano, red pepper, carrots, and olives. Cover and simmer until chicken is nearly tender. Add prunes and more pepper to taste. Cover and cook 10-15 minutes or until prunes are tender.
4-6 Servings

Peggy Neufeld
New Milford

Fernhouse Turkey Vegetable Chili

This is our favorite chili, low in salt, fat, and cholesterol, but hot and spicy. Keep a batch in the freezer, it's perfect for informal occasions any season. Serve over brown rice, pasta or coarsely mashed potatoes.

1 1/2 pounds hot or sweet turkey
    sausage
2 tablespoons olive oil
1 cup low-salt chicken broth
6 cloves garlic, minced
1 large onion, coarsely chopped
2 large carrots, coarsely chopped
2 stalks celery, coarsely chopped
1 1/2 pounds ground lean turkey
3/4 cup dry red wine (optional)
2 cups low-salt tomato sauce,
    fresh or canned

1 28-ounce can low-salt crushed
    tomatoes, drained, reserving
    liquid
Water
1 package Wick Fowler's 2 Alarm
    Chili Seasonings
1 large green pepper, seeded and
    coarsely chopped
1 19-ounce can kidney beans,
    drained and rinsed

Preheat oven to 375°. Bake sausage for 30 minutes to cook off fat. Cool. Slice into 1/4" rounds. Reserve. In 6 quart casserole, in olive oil and 1/2 cup broth, cook garlic, onions, carrots and celery for about five minutes, slowly adding other 1/2 cup broth as mixture cooks. Set vegetables aside. In the same casserole, retaining some liquid, barely brown ground turkey, separating it as it cooks. Stir in wine, tomato sauce, reserved tomato juice plus water to make 2 cups. Immediately stir in chili seasonings, discarding salt packet and reserving masa. Stir in sautéed vegetable mixture. Simmer for 45 minutes. Mix masa into 3/8 cup warm water, stirring until smooth. Add to chili. Add crushed tomatoes, simmer 10 minutes. Add green pepper, simmer 15 minutes. Add beans, simmer 5 minutes.

12 + Servings

Patricia and Kermit Adler
New Milford

Chicken with Bourbon and Chestnuts

In the autumn, use Litchfield Hills chestnuts to make this a truly special dish. The flavor is fantastic.

4 boneless chicken breast halves
Salt and pepper to taste
Flour
3-4 tablespoons olive oil
2 tablespoons finely chopped
  garlic
3 tablespoons finely chopped
  shallots

2 ounces fresh spinach, picked
  and washed
4 ounces Kentucky bourbon
2 ounces chicken stock
3/4 cup heavy cream
16 chestnuts, roasted and peeled

Season chicken breasts and dust with flour. Heat olive oil in sauté pan. When hot, add chicken and sauté until golden brown on both sides; remove from pan. Add garlic, shallots and spinach, and sauté for 1 minute. Flame with bourbon, add chicken stock and reduce by half. Return chicken to pan, add cream and chestnuts. Simmer 4-5 minutes, or until chicken is cooked and cream is reduced to sauce consistency. Pour sauce on plate, rest chicken on top and garnish with chestnuts and spinach.
4 Servings

E. Sayers and R. Epprecht, The Swiss Hospitality Institute
Washington

Lemon-Artichoke Chicken

A lovely, delicate zesty flavor. Serve with rice and a bright vegetable like carrots.

4 skinless, boneless chicken breast
  halves
1/4 cup butter
1 large garlic clove, minced
1/2 lemon, thinly sliced
1/2 pound fresh mushrooms,
  sliced

1 tablespoon flour
1 teaspoon salt
1/4 teaspoon fresh ground pepper
1/4 teaspoon dried oregano
1/2 cup dry white wine
1 14-ounce can whole artichoke
  hearts, drained and quartered

Pound breasts to 1/4" thickness. Cut into 2" squares. In large fry pan, heat butter over medium heat. Add chicken, cook 2-3 minutes on each side, until tender and opaque. Remove and keep warm. Add garlic, lemon and mushrooms to same pan. Cook until tender, 3-5 minutes. Sprinkle with flour, salt, pepper and oregano. Cook, stirring 1 minute. Add wine and bring to boil, stirring until mixture thickens. Add artichokes and return chicken to pan. Simmer 2 minutes until heated through.
4 Servings

Judith Burroughs
New Milford

Indian Style Chicken in Spiced Coconut Milk

Coconut milk and tamarind purée are found in Thai markets. Don't use coconut cream! Indian Style Basmati Rice is a perfect accompaniment.

2 bay leaves
1 cup canned coconut milk, divided
3¹/₂ pound chicken, cut into serving pieces
1 lemon, cut in half
1 small onion
4 macadamia nuts
2 slices ginger root, peeled and chopped
2 large garlic cloves, chopped
1 teaspoon ground coriander
¹/₄ teaspoon ground cumin
¹/₄ teaspoon turmeric
2 tablespoons peanut oil
1¹/₂ tablespoons tamarind purée
1 teaspoon sugar
1 teaspoon salt
¹/₄ teaspoon pepper
Scallion flowers
Cilantro sprigs

Preheat broiler. In small bowl soak bay leaves in coconut milk for one hour. Rinse, dry and trim chicken, rub both sides with cut side of lemon. Arrange chicken pieces skin side down on broiler pan. Broil 2" from heat for five minutes on each side, or until golden. Remove chicken. Turn off broiler; preheat oven to 350°. In food processor chop onion, macadamia nuts, ginger root, garlic, coriander, cumin and turmeric. With motor still running, add ¹/₂ cup coconut milk. Blend until smooth. In large baking pan heat peanut oil until hot. Add onion mixture and cook, stirring for 2 minutes. Stir in remaining coconut milk including bay leaves, adding tamarind purée, sugar, salt and pepper. Add chicken. Bake approximately 40 minutes, basting frequently, or until chicken is tender and liquid reduced to thick sauce. Garnish with scallion flowers and cilantro sprigs.
4 Servings

Liba Furhman
New Milford

Roast Chicken with Fennel

This dish is best if you can refrigerate the chicken spread with the garlic rosemary paste for 24 hours before roasting.

1 whole 3¹/₂ pound free-range or organic chicken	2 medium or 1 large fennel bulb
2 tablespoons extra virgin olive oil	1 large yellow onion
Freshly ground black pepper	¹/₂ cup dry white wine
3 large garlic cloves, crushed	¹/₂ cup "hot links" sausage, chopped
1¹/₂ tablespoons minced fresh rosemary	¹/₄ teaspoon salt

Wash and dry chicken, removing excess fat, reserving giblets. Cover with olive oil and black pepper. Using fork or mortar and pestle, mix garlic with rosemary to make paste. Spread mixture over chicken and place in 9"x13" glass baking dish. Preheat oven to 450°. Remove grassy top from fennel bulb; mince leaves finely, julienne the stems, and cut bulb lengthwise into ¹/₄" slices. Peel onion and cut into eighths lengthwise. Surround bird with sliced fennel bulb and onions. Bake 30 minutes. Reduce heat to 350° and pour wine over chicken. Scatter giblets, sausage and julienned fennel stems around chicken. Sprinkle chicken with salt. Return dish to oven. Baste every 15 minutes. Cook 45 minutes more, or until juices run clear. Remove from oven, sprinkle with minced green fennel top, let rest for 10 minutes.

4 Servings

Michael Chelminski
Bridgewater

Sour Cream Stuffed Chicken with New Potatoes

Make this a complete dinner by adding a fresh garden salad and white wine or Champagne.

1 roasting chicken	1 teaspoon Dijon mustard
¹/₂ lemon	Sweet butter
Salt and freshly ground pepper	Sesame oil
Fresh sage or basil, chopped	New potatoes
1 cup sour cream	

Preheat oven to 350°. Rub whole cleaned chicken with lemon, salt and pepper. Mix together 1 tablespoon chopped sage or basil, sour cream and mustard. Stuff chicken with mixture and close with toothpicks. Roast chicken 1 to 1¹/₂ hours, basting with mix of melted butter and sesame oil. About 45 minutes before chicken is done, add new potatoes coating them with pan juices. Sprinkle them with additional chopped sage or basil.

Diane von Furstenberg
New Milford

Bourbon Street Chicken

A Villager favorite! Nice served with wild rice pilaf.

2 large boneless, skinless chicken breast halves
1/2 cup all-purpose flour
Powdered Cajun spice mix to taste
2-3 tablespoons olive oil
1/2 cup white wine or chicken broth
1 tablespoon fresh tarragon, chopped
1/4 cup heavy cream
1/2 teaspoon Dijon mustard

Pound chicken breasts to 1/4" thickness, between sheets of waxed paper. Preheat 10-12" skillet over medium high heat. Combine flour and Cajun spice and rub into both sides of chicken. Add oil to skillet, heat to near smoking point and add chicken breasts. Cook 3 minutes per side or until firm, juices just running clear. Remove to warm plate. Add wine or stock to skillet, scraping up brown bits and cook until reduced by half. Add tarragon and cream and reduce until almost thick. Stir in mustard; pour sauce over chicken and serve.

2 Servings
Bill Leo, The Villager Restaurant
Kent

Stir Fried Chicken Strips with Vegetables

Though this is good any season, it's at its best with fresh local vegetables and home grown basil. It's fast, tasty, and kindly to those watching their cholesterol. Try it with turkey, too.

1/4 cup chicken broth
1/4 cup white wine Worcestershire sauce
1/2 teaspoon cornstarch
1/2 teaspoon dried basil, crushed
1/2 teaspoon garlic, minced
1/4 teaspoon onion powder
Dash cayenne pepper
2 tablespoons margarine
2 boneless, skinless chicken breast halves
1 1/2 cups mixed fresh broccoli, baby carrots, red peppers and water chestnuts
Chow mein or rice noodles

Stir together chicken broth, Worcestershire sauce, cornstarch, basil, garlic, onion powder and cayenne; set aside. Rinse chicken and pat dry. Cut chicken into 1/2" strips. In medium skillet, melt margarine. Sauté chicken over medium heat for 2-3 minutes, turning occasionally. Add vegetables. Cook while stirring, about 2 minutes more. Add chicken broth mixture, stirring as you pour it in. Continue stirring until thickened and bubbly, about 2 minutes more. Serve over noodles.

2 Servings
Sydell Brenner, Northville Supermarket
New Milford

Cheesy Chicken Enchiladas

The filling makes this recipe, so feel free to experiment. For more heat, fire it up with some diced jalapeños. Beef can be substituted for the chicken or eliminate the meat entirely for cheese enchiladas.

For sauce:
3 tablespoons vegetable oil
1¹/₂ cups chopped onion
3 teaspoons minced garlic
1¹/₂ teaspoons chili powder
1¹/₂ teaspoons oregano
1¹/₂ teaspoons cumin
³/₄ teaspoon salt
¹/₄ teaspoon ground pepper
1 28-ounce can plus 1 16-ounce
   can of whole tomatoes

For filling:
1¹/₂ cups shredded Cheddar
   cheese
1¹/₂ cups shredded Monterey Jack
   cheese
¹/₂ cup vegetable oil
2 cups shredded cooked chicken
   breast
12 small flour tortillas
Chopped lettuce, chopped tomato
   and sour cream for garnish

Heat oil in saucepan over medium heat. Add onion, garlic, and chili powder. Cook until onion is tender. Stir in next 5 ingredients. Bring to boil, reduce heat and simmer, uncovered, until thick, about 40 minutes. Preheat oven to 350°. Cover bottom of a 13"x9" baking dish with ¹/₄"-¹/₂" sauce. Combine cheeses. Set aside. Heat ¹/₂ cup of oil in skillet. Dip a tortilla in oil until just softened. Remove and fill tortilla with some of the cheese and chicken. Roll and place in the baking dish. Repeat with the other tortillas, reserving some cheese to put on top. Pour remaining sauce over the rolled tortillas, then sprinkle with cheese. Bake uncovered for 20 minutes. Garnish with lettuce, tomatoes and sour cream.
6 Servings

Kay Caroe
Woodbury

Chicken Legs Diable

These are delicious with corn bread and coleslaw.

4 whole chicken legs or 8 thighs
4 tablespoons butter
¹/₂ cup honey

¹/₄ cup prepared mustard
³/₄ teaspoon salt, or to taste
1 teaspoon curry powder

Preheat oven to 375°. Wash and dry chicken pieces. Melt butter in oven in baking pan large enough to accommodate the chicken in one layer. Stir honey, mustard, salt and curry into melted butter. Coat chicken with honey mixture, covering both sides well, and arrange in a single layer in the baking pan. Bake about 1 hour.
4 Servings

Ruth Diamond
New Milford

Juicy Orange Chicken

This is simple to prepare for a small group or a gang. Rice is a good accompaniment, since a lot of liquid is generated in the cooking. It makes a lovely light sauce.

Chicken pieces
Salt and freshly ground pepper to
    taste

Frozen orange juice concentrate,
    thawed
Navel orange slices

Preheat broiler. Place chicken in broiler pan, skin side up. Season chicken, then broil until nicely browned. Change oven temperature to Bake at 350°. Pour some thawed, undiluted orange juice on each chicken piece, then place a slice of orange on each. Cover pan with foil and bake until desired doneness.

Priscilla Manning Porter
Washington

Off the hook

splendid seafood dishes to lure
Bantam Lake fishermen, Housatonic anglers
and all those who can't resist the
catch of Connecticut.

Seared Mexican Shrimp
over Wasabi Scented Corn with Chives

I associate this recipe with my former restaurant. It's easy and everyone loves corn and shrimp. When chive blossoms are available, they make a beautiful garnish.

3 pounds Mexican shrimp
Olive oil
2 tablespoons sea salt
8 ears of fresh corn
$1/4$ pound sweet butter

1 tablespoon prepared wasabi
　powder (Japanese
　horseradish)
1 lemon, juice only
1 tablespoon snipped fresh chives

Peel shrimp, tail intact, devein and marinate in olive oil and salt. Set aside until ready to use. Remove corn husks and cut kernels from cob. Blanch corn in boiling water for 1 minute, drain and cool. Place shrimp in hot skillet, cook quickly over high heat on each side just until firm to the touch, remove to warm plate. Add butter to skillet, heat until foamy, add wasabi and lemon juice; mix well. Toss in blanched corn to heat and coat with wasabi butter. Stir in grilled shrimp and chives; taste for seasonings. Serve at once.
6 Servings

Carole Peck, Carole Peck Catering
New Preston

Fillet of Sole with Chopped Lemon and Capers

Quick, easy, healthy and a family favorite. Serve with boiled, red, new potatoes, tossed with butter and parsley.

2 sole fillets, preferably gray sole
3 tablespoons flour
1 teaspoon paprika
1 tablespoon olive oil
1 tablespoon butter

1 fresh lemon, peeled, seeded and
　coarsely chopped
2 tablespoons small capers
$1/3$ cup dry white wine

Dredge sole in mixture of flour and paprika. Shake off excess flour. Heat oil and butter in 8"-10" skillet, depending on size of fillets. Sauté over medium high heat about 2 minutes each side. Remove to warm platter. Add lemon, capers and wine to skillet, bring to boil, scraping up any bits on bottom of pan. Pour sauce over fillets and serve.
2 Servings

Marillyn R. Arturi
Kent

Steamed Mussels Bistro Style

You can tailor this recipe to your taste by adding capers or other herbs such as tarragon, fennel or thyme. French bread is a delicious tool for soaking up excess broth, or serve mussels over pasta. Small mussels, 1"-2" are best.

$^1/_4$ cup olive oil
1 tablespoon chopped garlic
$^1/_2$ tablespoon chopped shallots
$^1/_4$ cup leeks, julienned
48 cleaned mussels
1 cup ripe tomato or canned plum
    tomatoes, chopped
1 teaspoon chopped fresh
    rosemary

1 tablespoon chopped fresh basil
$^3/_4$ dry white wine
$^1/_2$ cup bottled clam juice
Kosher salt and white pepper
1 tablespoon butter
Sprig rosemary for garnish

Heat large sauté pan on high heat to very hot, at least 2 minutes. Add olive oil, garlic, shallots, leeks and mussels. Shake pan lightly for 15 seconds to be sure ingredients are cooked together. Add tomatoes, rosemary and basil. Sauté 15-20 seconds. Add wine, clam juice, salt and pepper. To create a dome so the mussels have sufficient room to open, cover pan with second, inverted sauté pan instead of lid. Simmer approximately 3 minutes until mussels have opened. Do not overcook; once they are open, they are done! Remove top pan, add butter and swirl until incorporated. Garnish.
2-4 Servings

Charles Bistro
New Milford

Swordfish with Champagne Dill Mustard Sauce

$^1/_3$ cup Italian dressing
2 swordfish or shark steaks, about
    1 pound
$^1/_2$ cup dry white wine

$^1/_8$ teaspoon pepper
1 tablespoon New England
    Champagne Dill Mustard
$^1/_2$ cup heavy cream

In large skillet, heat Italian dressing and cook fish over medium heat 8 minutes, turning once, or until fish flakes. Remove to serving platter and keep warm. Add wine to skillet, pepper and Champagne mustard. Bring to boil, then simmer, stirring occasionally, 8 minutes. Stir in cream and heat 1 minute or until thickened. Serve over fish.
2 Servings

Gourmet Products, Inc.
Watertown

Jonah Crab Corn Cakes with Jonah Crab Vinaigrette

For cakes:
3 cups clam juice
2 tablespoons shallots, minced
$^1/_2$ teaspoon garlic, minced
1 cup stone ground cornmeal
1 pound jonah crab meat
2 tablespoons parsley, minced
1 tablespoon chives, snipped
Sea salt, freshly ground white
    pepper,
Tabasco sauce
Canola oil pan spray

For vinaigrette:
8 ounces jonah crab meat
$^2/_3$ cup tomatoes, skinned
    deseeded and chopped
1 tablespoon green basil, minced
2 tablespoons parsley, minced
1 tablespoon shallot
2 teaspoons garlic, minced
$^1/_4$ cup lemon juice
$^3/_4$ cup grapeseed oil
Salt and crushed hot red pepper
    to taste.

Bring clam juice, shallots and garlic to boil. Whisk in corn meal and cook on low heat, 15 minutes. Fold in crab meat, minced herbs and season to taste. Bring back to boil and remove from heat. Fill 2 pieces of 2" diameter x $6^1/_2$" length PVC pipe with this mixture, wrap in plastic wrap and refrigerate. Make vinaigrette by mixing together all ingredients. Allow flavors to marry 30 minutes before serving. When ready to serve, push crab corn cake out of PVC pipe at 1" intervals and slice. Heat non-stick fry pan, spray with canola oil and brown cakes on both sides. Serve 3 cakes per person with small green salad, and pass the Jonah Crab Vinaigrette.
4 Servings

The Mayflower Inn
Washington

My Husband Henry's Ultra Easy Scallops

You can also add some white wine, but it's just as good without.

1 pound bay or sea scallops
Butter
Juice from one lemon
Jane's Krazy Salt

Pepper
Dried parsley flakes
Dried dill

Rinse scallops in strainer. Melt an inch of butter in frying pan. Squeeze lemon juice into butter, then sprinkle in Jane's Krazy Salt, parsley and dill. Turn heat to medium high and put in scallops. Keep turning them over and over for about 5 minutes until they shrink and tighten up — you'll be able to tell. Serve immediately with juices on rice or potatoes.
3-4 Servings

Polly Mellen
South Kent

Hearty Shrimp Creole

2 teaspoons minced onions
1 small green pepper, chopped
1 clove garlic, chopped
1 tablespoon chopped green celery
    tops
1/4 cup butter
2 1/2 cups canned tomatoes
4 slices bread
2 tablespoons sherry

2-3 cups raw, shelled shrimp,
    deveined
Salt and pepper to taste
Thyme, mace, nutmeg to taste
Bay leaves
3 hard-boiled eggs, coarsely
    chopped
Sherry to taste
2 cups croutons, lightly browned
    in butter

Cook onion, green pepper, garlic and celery in butter until barely browned. Add tomatoes and stir. Soak bread in 2 tablespoons sherry and add to mixture. Add shrimp and seasonings to taste. Bring to boil, reduce heat and simmer 10 minutes. Remove bay leaves. Add eggs and sherry to taste. Turn into casserole and top with croutons to serve.

Anne Plaut
New Milford

Simple Crab and Shrimp Casserole

This dish can be assembled ahead so you'll be free to join your guests while it cooks during the cocktail hour.

1 1/2 pounds crab meat
1/2-1 pound large whole shrimp,
    cooked and peeled
1/2 green pepper, cut in 1" strips
1 1/2 cups mayonnaise

2 cups boiled rice, slightly
    undercooked
2 packages frozen peas, thawed
Salt and pepper to taste

Preheat oven to 350°. Mix all ingredients, except shrimp and place in lightly greased casserole. Arrange shrimp in a decorative pattern on top. Cover casserole and bake 1 hour.
6 Servings

Joan DeWind
Sherman

Stoccafisso Marinara

This is a traditional recipe of the Riviera, both the French and Italian coasts. There, it's most often made with stockfish. Salt cod can also be used (after soaking); here I've used fresh cod.

1 medium onion, finely chopped
8 ounces extra-virgin olive oil
3 cloves garlic, each cut into 2 or 3 pieces
8 small russet potatoes, half-boiled, then peeled and cut into chunks
1 35-ounce can peeled Italian tomatoes, lightly mashed with fork

1 teaspoon Knorr fish broth (powder)
4 ounces Gaeta olives, pitted
3 tablespoons finely chopped parsley
2 3-inch "strings" anchovy paste from tube
5 bay leaves
1/3 cup milk
2 pounds fresh cod fillet, cut in 2"-3" pieces

In large ovenproof casserole (enameled cast iron or terra-cotta), gently cook onion in about 3 tablespoons olive oil, until wilted, about 3 minutes. Add garlic; sauté another minute. Add remaining ingredients, except fish and simmer very gently for an hour over low heat. Cool and let sit, covered, in refrigerator overnight. Preheat oven to 375°. Mix fish into casserole and bake, uncovered, for about an hour.
Serves 6

**Arthur Schwartz
Cornwall**

Maine Lobster Stew

An elegant summer supper, served with pilot crackers or homemade bread.

1 medium onion	Dill, chopped
2 tablespoons butter or ¹/₈ pound salt pork	Parsley, chopped
	1 cup milk
¹/₂ pound lobster meat, cooked	1 cup evaporated milk
Salt and pepper to taste	Paprika

In a small, heavy saucepan, sauté onion in butter or salt pork cut into tiny cubes until the mixture begins to color. Add salt, pepper, dill, parsley and both milks. Simmer, do not boil, for approximately 15 minutes. Add lobster; heat through. Sprinkle with paprika.
2 Servings

Audrey Patterson
New Preston

Broiled Fresh Atlantic Salmon

This recipe requires fresh, farm-raised Atlantic salmon. Fresh, because it tastes best and farm-raised, because the glorious Atlantic salmon is in trouble in the wild. Fortunately, the dedication of such groups as the Atlantic Salmon Foundation and the Restoration of the Atlantic Salmon are helping greater numbers of fish to return to the ocean and their home rivers.

1 whole Atlantic salmon, 6-7 pounds	Additional lemon juice
	Garlic, minced
White wine, lemon juice and fish spice to taste	

Scale fish with dull paring knife or fish scaler (outdoors, because the scales fly all over the place). Remove fins and yellowish bit of meat near belly. Cut into 1"-2" steaks. Marinate in white wine, lemon juice and fish spices for a few hours. When ready to cook, arrange steaks on oiled broiler pan. Squeeze ¹/₂ the lemon juice on top and spread on ¹/₂ the garlic. Broil 3"-4" from heat for 4-5 minutes. Turn. Apply rest of lemon juice and garlic. Broil 4-5 minutes more.
8-10 Servings

Robert A. Oden, Jr., Headmaster, The Hotchkiss School
Lakeville

Traditional Shellfish Pie

1¹/₂ pounds scallops
³/₄ pound shrimp
Butter
1 cup onion, chopped
1 cup celery, chopped
1 tablespoon garlic
1 cup sherry

Flour
Chicken base to taste
Thyme to taste
¹/₂ pound crab, cooked
4 ounces lobster, cooked
2 large mushrooms
Puff pastry for topping

Poach scallops and shrimp; reserve liquid. Sauté onions, celery, garlic in butter. Add flour to create roux. Add sherry and enough poaching liquid to make a velouté sauce. Season with chicken base and thyme. Add all shellfish and let cool. Place in individual casserole dishes with a mushroom quarter. Top with puff pastry and garnish with cut ¹/₂ moons of puff pastry. Bake until golden brown, 15-20 minutes.
8 Servings

Tollgate Hill Inn and Restaurant
Litchfield

Grilled Seafood Kabobs

Be sure to soak the bamboo skewers in water overnight before they are used in this recipe.

3 lemons, seeded
2 cups white wine
8 sprigs fresh dill
1¹/₄ cups olive oil
6 cloves garlic
¹/₄ cup Worcestershire sauce
Salt and pepper to taste

2¹/₂ pounds swordfish
2¹/₂ pounds tuna
2 red peppers
1 yellow pepper
1 red onion
2 pounds large, raw shrimp, peeled

Chop first 7 ingredients in food processor until a coarse purée results. Reserve in wide shallow bowl. Cut swordfish, tuna, peppers and red onion into large cubes and alternate with shrimp on skewers. Dip each kabob into marinade and stack in pan, pouring excess marinade over top. Allow to stand, refrigerated, at least 3 hours before grilling.
10-12 Servings

Michael Ackerman, The Pantry
Washington Depot

Grapevine Smoked Salmon Fillet

This recipe was prepared for a winery dinner by the executive chef of the Tollgate Hill Inn. We used Haight wine (Recolte) and our own grapevines for smoking. The chef earned well-deserved praise that night.

1 pound Haight grapevines	3 ounces heavy cream
4 7-ounce salmon fillets	8 ounces butter
1 ounce shallots	Salt and pepper to taste
2 cups Recolte wine	2 ounces sundried grapes

Smoke salmon: soak grapevines in water for $1/2$ hour. Remove from water and place in deep metal pan. Place perforated pan over vines and cover with lid. Turn on high heat until smoke appears, approximately 5 minutes. Place salmon on top of perforated pan and cover. Cook for approximately 5-8 minutes. Remove from smoker and keep warm. Make sauce: in saucepan, combine shallots and wine. Reduce by $3/4$. Add cream, reduce by $1/2$ and let cool down slightly. Whisk in softened butter, salt and pepper. Add sundried grapes. Serve over freshly smoked salmon.
4 Servings

Sherman P. Haight, Jr., Haight Vineyard
Litchfield

On the hoof

the best beef, veal, pork and lamb dishes
to tempt Steep Rock Park cross-country skiers,
Bridgewater barbecuers and
all happy guests who ask for more!

Purple Pork Roast

This roast is made in a clay baker or "Schlemmertopf", an easy, fool-proof way to cook. The meat and vegetables cook in their own juices with no extra fat. The flavor is out of this world. Have your butcher cut through the bone to create 6 loosely attached chops.

3 red apples, cored and sliced
Juice of 2 lemons
12 prunes
1 3½-pound center-cut pork
    roast, with bone
Salt and freshly ground black
    pepper

4 ounces prepared honey mustard
1 head red cabbage, shredded
2 tablespoons light brown sugar
2 tablespoons balsamic vinegar
1 teaspoon dried marjoram
6 baking potatoes
1 onion, studded with 30 cloves

Sprinkle apples with half the lemon juice, set aside. Place prunes in medium bowl, cover with water and soak 30 minutes. Wash and dry meat thoroughly. Sprinkle with remaining lemon juice, salt and pepper. Spread honey mustard over outside of roast and in between chops. Set aside. Combine cabbage, apples, brown sugar, vinegar and marjoram in "Schlemmertopf". Toss well. Place pork on top of bed of cabbage. Arrange potatoes, onion and prunes around meat. Cover and place in cold oven. Set temperature to 425°. Roast 2 hours.
6 Servings

Ruth and Skitch Henderson, The Silo
New Milford

Charcoal Grilled Lamb Chops with Fresh Mint

Simple and scrumptious!

4 loin lamb chops, 1" thick
¼ cup lemon juice
¼ cup chopped fresh mint leaves
1 teaspoon grated lemon rind

¼ teaspoon sugar
½ teaspoon salt
⅓ cup olive oil

Trim fat from chops and make several slits around edges. Pour lemon juice into blender. Add mint leaves, lemon rind, sugar and salt. Blend at high speed 5 seconds, add olive oil and mix well. Marinate chops, turning frequently to coat thoroughly. Let stand at least 1 hour at room temperature to marry flavors, turning occasionally. Remove chops from mint sauce and grill over medium hot coals for 7-8 minutes on each side, basting with sauce.
2 Servings

Kathryn Popper
South Kent

Butterflied Leg of Lamb in Lemon Garlic Marinade

One of the best company dishes ever. Be sure the lamb is of the highest quality, perhaps from one of our local farms.

6-7 pound leg of lamb, boned
$^2/_3$ cup olive oil
3 tablespoons lemon juice
1 teaspoon salt
Freshly ground pepper

2 tablespoons minced parsley
1 teaspoon dry oregano
3 bay leaves, crumbled
1 cup onions, thinly sliced
3 cloves garlic, thinly sliced

Trim excess fat from lamb. Make a few slashes so meat will lie flat. (The thickness will vary, resulting in both rare and well done meat.) Pierce lamb several times with fork. Lay flat in pan, preferably cast iron, $1^1/_2$" deep. Combine remaining ingredients for marinade. Marinate 24 hours in refrigerator, turning several times. Bring to room temperature before cooking. Preheat broiler. Leaving marinade in pan, broil lamb about 4" from heat, approximately 15 minutes on each side. Slice and serve with a spoonful of marinade, removing bay leaves.
8-10 Servings

Rita Easton
Sharon

Oxtail Ragout

For a large group, triple the oxtails and double the other ingredients. Serve with broad noodles.

$2^1/_2$ pounds disjointed oxtails
3 tablespoons cooking oil
1 teaspoon salt
$^1/_4$ teaspoon freshly ground
    pepper
8 whole allspice

1 bay leaf
1 stalk celery
1 small onion, peeled
$1^1/_2$ cups water
1 cup red wine
1 tablespoon cornstarch

Wash and dry oxtails. In heavy pan, brown in oil on all sides. Add next 7 ingredients. Cover tightly and simmer 2 hours or until meat leaves bone easily. Add wine and simmer 10 minutes longer. Using slotted spoon, remove meat from liquid and keep warm. Skim fat from liquid in pan. Mix a little water with cornstarch to form paste. Add paste to pan and stir over low heat until gravy thickens. Return oxtails to pan and heat. Serve with gravy.
4 Servings

Ruth Diamond
New Milford

Fool Proof Filet with Béarnaise Sauce

1 whole beef filet, completely
    trimmed
Garlic powder
Salt
Freshly ground black pepper
For Béarnaise sauce:
1 tablespoon minced green onion
    or shallots
$^1/_4$ teaspoon white pepper
$^1/_2$ teaspoon tarragon leaves

$^1/_2$ teaspoon chervil
$2^1/_2$ tablespoons red wine vinegar
$2^1/_2$ tablespoons Chablis
3 egg yolks
2 tablespoons water
$^1/_2$ cup butter, melted
$^1/_4$ cup finely chopped parsley
1 teaspoon lemon juice
Salt to taste

Preheat oven to 450°. Season meat with salt, pepper and garlic powder. Roast 25-30 minutes. Meat thermometer should read 120° for medium rare. For sauce: combine first 6 ingredients in top of double boiler. Simmer over direct heat until almost all liquid is evaporated. Beat yolks and water; add to pot. Place over hot water and cook until thick and creamy. Place into food processor and add butter slowly with machine running. Add parsley, lemon juice and salt to taste.
Yield: Filet with 1 cup sauce

Barbara Brinton, Corner Country Kitchen, Inc.
Washington Depot

Veal Scallopine with Cheese and Madeira Sauce

2 pounds veal scallops, sliced thin
    and lightly breaded
8 tablespoons butter, divided
3 tablespoons Madeira
$^1/_2$ cup water
$^1/_2$ cup milk

1 bouillon cube
1 tablespoon flour
$^1/_4$ teaspoon nutmeg
Freshly ground pepper
$^1/_2$ pound Gruyère or
    Emmenthaler cheese, grated

Heat 6 tablespoons butter in skillet over medium heat. Add veal and cook until browned on both sides. Remove veal to warm platter. Add Madeira to skillet and cook a few seconds, scraping particles from bottom of pan. Set skillet aside. Preheat oven to 425°. Make sauce: bring water and milk to boil in saucepan and dissolve bouillon cube in mixture. In another small saucepan, melt remaining 2 tablespoons butter, add flour and stir with wire whisk until blended. Add water-milk mixture all at once, stirring constantly until thickened, blended and smooth. Add nutmeg and pepper. Arrange veal in single layer in shallow baking dish. Pour sauce over veal and top with grated cheese. Heat until cheese melts.
6 Servings

Governor Lowell Weicker, Jr.
Hartford

Egg and I Farm Chili

Simple and satisfying on a cold night around the fire. Of course, the better the pork, the better the chili, and nothing beats fresh from the farm.

1 pound ground pork	1 bay leaf
1 onion, chopped	1 teaspoon Worcestershire sauce
1 green pepper, chopped	2 8-ounce cans tomato sauce
1 teaspoon salt	2 16-ounce cans kidney beans,
1-2 teaspoons chili powder	drained

In skillet, break up pork with fork and cook until lightly browned. Pour off excess fat. In pot, combine meat with onion, pepper, salt, chili powder, bay leaf, Worcestershire sauce, tomato sauce, and kidney beans. Cover and cook on low heat $2^1/_2$ hours. Remove bay leaf.
6-7 Servings

Jim and Nancy Dougherty, The Egg and I Farm
New Milford

Honeyed Oriental Pork Chops

2 tablespoons vegetable oil	1 tablespoon sesame seeds
1 clove garlic, minced	$^3/_4$ teaspoon Tabasco
4 tablespoons minced ginger root	4 pork chops, 1" thick
$^1/_2$ cup dry sherry	1 teaspoon cornstarch
$^1/_2$ cup soy sauce	2 tablespoons water
$^1/_4$ cup honey	Orange slices, cut into quarters
1 tablespoon grated orange peel	

Heat oil in medium saucepan. Add garlic and ginger; cook 1 minute. Remove from heat; add next 6 ingredients and mix well. Add chops to marinade. Refrigerate 1 hour, turning occasionally. When ready to serve, preheat grill or broiler. Remove chops from marinade; pour marinade into small saucepan. Grill chops 10 minutes on each side. Meanwhile, in small bowl combine cornstarch and water; stir into marinade. Bring to boil over medium heat, stirring constantly. Boil 1 minute. Brush chops with marinade. Grill 5-10 minutes longer or until done, turning and brushing frequently. Serve with remaining marinade and garnish with orange slices.
4 Servings

Gourmet Products, Inc.
Watertown

Beef à la Dutch

This is a lovely, old-fashioned dish, delicious on a bed of buttered rice.

1 pound sirloin strip steak, cut
   into $^1/_2$" cubes
2 tablespoons olive oil
Flour, mixed with salt and pepper
1 clove garlic, chopped
1 cup sliced mushrooms

$^1/_2$ cup chopped onions
$^1/_2$ cup red wine
$^1/_2$ cup heavy cream
1 teaspoon Bovril beef concentrate
Salt and pepper to taste
2 teaspoons butter

Heat large skillet to moderate heat. Add oil. Flour meat and sauté 4 minutes; add garlic, mushrooms and onion. Continue sautéing until onions and mushrooms are wilted, about 2 minutes. Add wine and stir; cook 1 minute. Add heavy cream and beef concentrate, continue stirring until thickened. Taste and correct seasonings. It should have a rich beef flavor. Add butter and stir just before serving.
4 Servings

John Harney
Salisbury

Stuffed Veal Shoulder

$3^1/_2$-4 pound veal shoulder, boned
3 tablespoons olive oil, divided
4 thick slices stale Italian bread,
   crust removed
1 cup stuffing mix
2 tablespoons grated Romano
   cheese
1 clove garlic, crushed
1 tablespoon raisins

1 tablespoon pine nuts
2 tablespoons chopped Italian
   parsley
Salt and pepper to taste
Flour
1 cup dry white wine
1 cup chicken broth
3 bay leaves

Preheat oven to 425°. Spread veal open and brush lightly with 1 tablespoon olive oil. In food processor, coarsely process bread. Add stuffing mix, cheese, garlic, raisins, pine nuts, parsley, salt and pepper. Process until just blended, not too fine. Spread filling over meat, roll and tie securely. In heavy skillet, heat 2 tablespoons olive oil. Roll meat in flour, then brown in hot oil. Place meat on rack in roasting pan so it will sit above, not in, the liquid. Add wine, broth and bay leaves. Roast, uncovered, for $^1/_2$ hour. Reduce temperature to 325°, cover and braise for 2 hours or until tender. Remove from oven and let rest 15 minutes. Remove string and slice. Juices can be thickened or served as is.
6-8 Servings

Mary Cortina
New Milford

Barbecued Baby-Back Ribs

Perfect for a summer evening with sangria, guacamole, cornbread, cole-slaw and fresh strawberry shortcake. These ribs are at their absolute finest if you have time to marinate them in the sauce overnight.

18 pieces baby-back ribs
3 tablespoons butter
1/2 cup minced onion
1/2 cup minced celery
1 garlic clove, minced
1/4 teaspoon cumin
3 tablespoons brown sugar
2 tablespoons cider vinegar

1 cup ketchup
1 cup beef broth
2 teaspoons Worcestershire sauce
2 teaspoons Dijon mustard
1/2 teaspoon cayenne
Salt and pepper to taste
1 tablespoon fresh lime juice

In large skillet, cook onion, celery, and garlic in butter over moderate heat until soft. Add remaining ingredients, except lime juice, stir, bring to a boil, then simmer 30 minutes. Add lime juice last. Grill ribs over medium hot charcoal fire, making sure they don't cook too quickly. Avoid letting them flame up, if possible. Baste often with sauce. Keep plenty of sauce in reserve. When ribs are cooked and still sizzling off the fire, plunge them into remaining sauce to get full expression of meat and sauce. Serve on large platter, spooning on any extra sauce.
6 Servings

**Dan Dwyer
Salisbury**

Veal Scallops with Apples and Cream

3 2-ounce veal scallops
Salt and pepper
Flour
Clarified butter
1/2 Granny Smith apple, sliced
3 medium mushrooms, sliced
1 tablespoon Calvados

1 ounce apple juice
1 ounce demi-glace, or beef or
    chicken stock
2 ounces heavy cream
1/2 teaspoon butter
Parsley, chopped

Season veal with salt and pepper; dredge with flour. Sauté in clarified butter, keeping on the pink side. Do not overcook. Flame with Calvados. Remove veal to warm plate. In same pan, add sliced apple and mushrooms; cook for a few minutes. Add apple juice and stock, reduce for few minutes. Add heavy cream and reduce until sauce is thickened. Adjust seasoning. Stir butter into sauce and pour over veal. Sprinkle with chopped parsley.
1 Serving

**Gérard Coyac, Le Marmiton
New Milford**

Potters Field Farm Veal Stew

We raise veal on our farm and dislike it overcooked or over-sauced. This classic dish is good with rice and a simple vegetable platter. It tastes best when made a day ahead.

2 pounds boneless veal, bite-sized
10 small white onions, peeled
Butter for browning
2 tablespoons flour
1 cup hot bouillon
2 tablespoons tomato paste
Salt and pepper to taste
Parsley bouquet
1 pound mushrooms, stems and
　caps separated
1 can artichoke hearts, drained
1 cup dry white wine
1 cup sour cream, optional

In 4 quart heavy pan or casserole, brown veal and onions in butter. Sprinkle with flour and stir until flour is browned. Add hot bouillon, tomato paste, seasonings and parsley. Cook slowly 30 minutes. Slice mushroom stems, leave caps whole; cut artichokes in half and add to casserole. Add wine. Cook 30 minutes longer. Correct seasonings and serve. Sour cream may be added just before serving. Recipe may be doubled or quadrupled if separate pots are used for browning.
8 Servings

Jean F. Potter, Potters Field Farm
Washington

Sugar Hill Farm Charcoal Grilled Leg of Lamb

This is our absolute favorite for grilling and guests love it. The honey used is sold in our farm store. We like the lamb pink, in thin slices, with tiny parsleyed potatoes from our garden.

5-7 pound boned and butterflied
　leg of lamb
3/4 cup hot water
1/4 cup honey
1/3 cup soy sauce
2 tablespoons salad oil
2 tablespoons lemon juice
4 garlic cloves, crushed
Red wine vinegar

Open up leg of lamb and trim away any excess fat. Mix next six ingredients in 2 cup measure. Add red wine vinegar to reach 2 cup mark and pour over lamb. Refrigerate, turning periodically, 8 hours or more, before cooking. When ready to cook, remove lamb from marinade and place flat on hot grill. Cook uncovered, about 10 minutes. Turn and cook for 10 minutes more. Time will vary according to degree of doneness desired. Let meat stand 10-15 minutes before serving.
6-8 Servings

Janice Sternlieb, Sugar Hill Farm
Colebrook

Grilled Rib-Eye Steak
with Crispy Gorgonzola Crust and Grilled Scallions

The sharpness of the cheese and scallions combine beautifully with the rich flavor of the steak.

4 8-10-ounce rib-eye steaks
1 tablespoon olive oil
Kosher salt and white pepper
1 tablespoon minced garlic
1 tablespoon minced shallots

1 large bunch scallions
$^1/_2$ pound Gorgonzola or other
   blue cheese
$^1/_4$ cup unseasoned breadcrumbs

Heat grill to very hot. Brush steaks with olive oil and season on both sides with salt, pepper, garlic and shallots. Grill steaks to desired doneness, turning once. Remove steaks from grill to broiler-proof pan. Preheat broiler. Brush scallions with oil and sprinkle with salt and pepper. Grill scallions until lightly browned. Remove scallions to warm plates. Crumble cheese, then bread crumbs on steaks. Broil steaks until cheese mixture is lightly browned. Serve steaks on top of grilled scallions.
4 Servings

Charles Bistro
New Milford

Pot Roast with Apple Cider

This recipe is perfect for apple season. I have served it successfully at dinner parties, accompanied with cider instead of wine for those who don't drink alcohol.

4 pounds beef chuck roast
1 large onion, sliced
8 whole cloves
2" piece ginger root, peeled and
   sliced
2 cinnamon sticks

$1^1/_2$ teaspoons salt
3-4 cups apple cider
2 tablespoons oil
8-10 small whole potatoes
1 pound bag frozen baby onions
16 baby carrots, peeled

Put beef, onion, cloves, ginger root, cinnamon sticks and salt into deep bowl. Pour in enough cider to cover completely, cover and refrigerate overnight, turning once. Strain marinade and reserve. Heat oil in Dutch oven and brown meat thoroughly on all sides. Add marinade, cover and simmer 1 hour. Add vegetables and simmer another 1 to $1^1/_2$ hours or until tender. Remove meat and vegetables to warm platter. Reduce pan juices and serve over thinly sliced meat.
8 Servings

Marjorie Owens
Bethel

Savory Pork Loin in Wine Marinade

This is an easy entrée for a big group that tastes remarkably like wild boar. The pork loin can be roasted in the oven, but it's spectacular slow-roasted on an outdoor grill. Serve with polenta or grits soufflé.

5-7 pound boneless rolled pork
  loin
2 tablespoons salt
$^1/_2$ cup olive oil
2 cups dry white wine
1 cup wine vinegar
4 garlic cloves, crushed
1 cup carrots, thinly sliced
1 cup yellow onions, sliced

1 teaspoon peppercorns
2 bay leaves
2 teaspoons thyme
1 teaspoon basil
1 teaspoon tarragon
1 teaspoon sage
5 coriander seeds
10 juniper berries

Rub salt into pork. Mix all other ingredients in large bowl. Add meat and baste. Refrigerate, covered, for at least 2 days, turning every day. When ready to roast, preheat oven to 325°. Remove meat from marinade and pat dry. Roast until internal temperature is 180-185°.
12-15 Servings

Julie Swaner, The Cobble Cookery
Kent

Classic No-Bean Chili

Serve with rice and pinto beans on the side.

5 pounds beef chuck, cubed
$^1/_2$ cup olive oil
$^1/_2$ cup flour
$^1/_2$ cup hot chili powder
2 tablespoons cumin seeds

2 tablespoons oregano leaves
6-8 garlic cloves, minced
4 cups beef broth
Salt and pepper to taste

Cook meat in olive oil until it loses its red color. Don't worry about browning the meat. It will probably just turn gray. Mix flour and chili powder and sprinkle on meat. Stir to coat thoroughly. Add cumin seeds, oregano, and garlic. Add 4 cups beef broth. Simmer 3-4 hours. Season with salt and pepper to taste.
8-10 Servings

Nancy Novogrod
Woodbury

Alice's Beef Carbonnade

Even the aroma of this hearty stew seems to ease winter's chill. One of my mother's favorites, it evokes memories of snowy days. My family loves to return from skiing and smell it simmering on the woodstove.

2 pounds cubed stew beef
$^1/_4$-$^1/_3$ cup flour
2 teaspoons salt
1 teaspoon freshly ground pepper
3 or more tablespoons oil, divided
1 clove garlic, crushed
6 large onions, thickly sliced
12 ounces beer

2 teaspoons Worcestershire sauce
3 bay leaves
1 tablespoon brown sugar
$^1/_2$ teaspoon ground thyme
3-4 medium potatoes, unpeeled, thickly sliced
1 pound peas, optional
Parsley garnish

Dredge beef with flour, salt and pepper. In large pot, sauté garlic and onion in oil until soft, then remove. In same pot, sauté beef until brown in more oil. Reduce heat, add sautéed onions and garlic, beer and seasonings. Simmer, covered, on very low heat about 2 hours, adding potatoes during last hour and peas during last 15 minutes. Adjust seasonings and garnish.
5 Servings

Lee Rush
New Milford

Flank on a Plank

This steak dish is made ahead, then served cold in thin, diagonal slices on French bread. Surrounded by watercress and sliced radishes, it looks pretty for brunch, supper or as an hors d'oeuvre.

$1^1/_2$ pounds flank steak
$^1/_3$ cup soy sauce
$^1/_3$ cup dark rum
2 tablespoons salad oil

For garnish:
Baguette slices
Watercress
Radish slices

Trim excess fat from steak, and wipe with damp paper towel. Combine soy sauce and rum in large shallow dish. Add steak. Refrigerate covered, turning occasionally, for 24 hours. Remove steak from marinade; brush lightly with oil. Place in broiler pan without rack. Broil 6" from heat 6 minutes on each side. Let cool; brush with pan juices. Refrigerate, lightly covered, until serving. Cut thinly on diagonal, place on bread and serve with garnish.
6-8 Servings

Barbara Hamlin
Litchfield

Braised Veal with Fresh Vegetables

3 pound roast of veal (shoulder or
    rump), boned and tied
2 tablespoons butter
Salt and pepper to taste
1 cup tomato juice
1 cup chicken stock
An herb bouquet of parsley
    sprigs, 1 bay leaf, $1/4$ teaspoon
    thyme, $1/4$ teaspoon
    Rosemary, tied in cheesecloth

6 medium carrots, pared and cut
    in chunks
2 medium onions, finely chopped
2 stalks celery, finely chopped
6 medium parsnips, pared and cut
    in chunks
3 cups mushrooms
6 large tomatoes, peeled or
    canned

Preheat oven to 325°. Brown veal in butter on all sides for 10-15 minutes. Remove from casserole and discard butter. Sprinkle veal with salt and pepper, return to casserole, add tomato juice, chicken stock and herb bouquet, along with carrots, onion and celery. Cover casserole and cook about 1 hour, basting several times with juices. After 1 hour add parsnips and mushrooms. Cook 20 minutes. Add tomatoes, cook another 15 minutes, no longer or they will disintegrate. Veal is done when juices run clear when pricked with fork. Place on hot platter, arranging vegetables around veal. Remove herb bouquet from casserole and set over moderate heat. Boil to reduce pan juices while scraping sides and bottom of pan. Pour juices into gravy boat and serve with veal.
6 Servings

Barbara Taylor Bradford

Fruited Lamb Shanks

This dish has been requested by my family for over 35 years.

4 lamb shanks, trimmed
3 large garlic cloves, crushed
2 tablespoons vegetable oil
12 ounces mixed dried fruit
$1/2$ cup sugar
$1/4$ cup vinegar

$1/2$ teaspoon cinnamon
$1/2$ teaspoon allspice
$1/2$ teaspoon cloves
$3/4$ teaspoon salt
3 cups water
Salt and pepper to taste

In large pan or Dutch oven, sauté lamb and garlic in oil until lamb has browned evenly. Drain fat from pan and discard. Add remaining ingredients and cook, covered, over low heat until tender.
4 Servings

**Ruth Diamond
New Milford**

Succulent Barbecued Spareribs

This has a thin sauce, distinctively flavored with chili powder and brushed on the meat just before serving. Serve with hot biscuits, coleslaw and sweet potato pie.

5 pounds pork spareribs
1 cup water
2 tablespoons fresh lemon juice
$^1/_4$ cup dry mustard
$^1/_4$ cup chili powder
1 tablespoon sugar

1 tablespoon paprika
2 teaspoons salt
1 teaspoon onion powder
1 teaspoon garlic powder
$^1/_4$ teaspoon cayenne pepper

Place spareribs in broiler pan, cover with foil and roast at 400° for $1^1/_2$ hours. Meanwhile, combine all sauce ingredients in medium saucepan; mix well. Bring to boil. Reduce heat; simmer for 30 minutes. Brush sauce on ribs. Broil 5" from heat for 7-10 minutes on each side. Serve ribs with additional sauce.
6 Servings

Jim and Nancy Dougherty, The Egg and I Farm
New Milford

Veal à la Suisse

3 pounds veal strips, 3"x$^1/_2$"
Salt and ground white pepper
Paprika
$^1/_2$ cup oil
$^1/_2$ cup white wine

1 cup sliced, cooked mushrooms
2 ounces Emmenthaler cheese
1 cup light cream
1 ounce cornstarch
Water

Season veal with salt, pepper and paprika. Heat oil in large frying pan. Add veal and sauté until lightly brown. Add white wine and enough water to just cover meat. Let simmer until tender, about 15 minutes. Add mushrooms, cheese and light cream. Then thicken sauce with cornstarch dissolved in small amount of water.
4-6 Servings

Rudy's Restaurant
New Milford

It's all in the game

venison, rabbit, wild mushrooms, duck,
pheasant, quail, fiddleheads in delectable dishes
to enjoy after exploring our scenic
roads and covered bridges.

Quail with Hazelnuts

Native Americans knew the special properties of wood ashes as an ingredient. Ashes add flavor and aid digestion. Spoon fresh ashes from your fireplace, woodstove or campfire. Don't scrape out the ashes or you'll get unwanted tar and residue.

4 quail, dressed
1/4 cup sunflower seed oil
1 cup fine cornmeal
1/4 cup nut butter of choice
1 cup hot water

1 teaspoon wood ashes
1 cup wild grapes, seeded
1/2 cup shelled hazelnuts,
    chopped
Rice or greens

Rub quail inside and out with oil and roll in cornmeal to coat skin lightly. Melt nut butter in skillet and sauté quail, turning often, until well browned. Add water, ashes and grapes. Cover, and simmer over low heat 45 minutes, stirring once or twice to blend. Meanwhile, preheat oven to 350°. Toast hazelnuts in shallow pan in oven until light brown, 10 minutes. Serve each quail on bed of rice or tender greens. Spoon toasted hazelnuts over each bird.
4 Servings

Barrie Kavasch
Bridgewater

Shaggy Mane Soup

Shaggy Mane, like other unique and flavorful wild mushrooms, are always a thrill to find growing along roadsides. This soup has been a delicious start to many holiday meals, and makes a warm, healthy meal on a cool autumn day.

1/2 cup American cheese
2 chicken bouillon cubes
1 cup chicken stock
3 cups Shaggy Mane mushrooms,
    finely chopped

2 tablespoons butter
2 tablespoons cornstarch or flour
3 1/2 cups milk
Pepper

In 2 quart saucepan, dissolve cheese and bouillon cubes in hot chicken stock. Add Shaggy Manes to stock and let simmer, covered, 35 minutes. In separate pan, melt butter and whisk in flour. Add to stock, whisking constantly. Stir in milk. Add pepper to taste.
4-6 Servings

Odilia Hylwa
Connecticut Mycology Society

Venison Swedish Meatballs

Serve these tasty morsels as an hors d'oeuvre or over rice as an entrée.

1 cup milk or water
3 eggs, beaten
4 slices white or whole wheat
    bread
2 pounds ground venison
1 medium onion, minced

2 teaspoons salt
$1/4$ cup butter, melted
$1/2$ teaspoon ground allspice
Pinch of ground ginger
Milk or water for sauce
1 tablespoon cornstarch

Preheat oven to 350°. In large mixing bowl, combine milk and eggs, add bread. When thoroughly soaked, add next 6 ingredients, mixing with hands to combine. Shape into 1" balls. Place in large, shallow roasting pan and bake 20 minutes. Transfer meatballs to large casserole. Heat roasting pan on stove top, adding liquid while scraping up brown bits. Stir cold water into cornstarch and add to liquid, stirring constantly until thickened. Pour over meatballs and serve.
Yield: 75 meatballs

Astrid Colvin
Washington Depot

Warren's Original Black Birch Dandelion Wine

Everyone knows about tapping maple trees, but in mid to late April you can also tap black birch. Tuck away a gallon of sap until a nice day in early May when the dandelions are in profusion.

2 quarts dandelion blossoms
1 lemon, sliced
1 orange, sliced
1 gallon black birch sap

3-4 pounds white sugar
$1/2$ ounce baker's or wine yeast
1 slice toasted bread

Wash blossoms thoroughly and put in large bowl or crock with sliced fruit. Bring sap to boil, pour over blossoms and stir well. Cover and let sit 10 days, stirring occasionally. Strain liquid into another crock and stir in sugar. Add yeast and float on a slice of toast. Cover and let sit several days. Remove toast and strain liquid into gallon jug to ferment. Top loosely with cork so air may escape. Leave several weeks, pouring it out occasionally, to remove sediment. When clear, 6-8 weeks, bottle and seal.

Peggy Koehler
New Milford

Tame Game Pot Pie

1 5-pound duckling
3/4 tablespoon dried thyme
Salt and pepper
1 2-pound rabbit
1/2 cup black currant vinegar
1/8 cup Dijon mustard
Flour
2 tablespoons oil, divided
1 cup red wine, divided
1/4 pound bacon

Garlic
1 pound pork
1 cup chopped onion
1/2 pound mushrooms, quartered
3 tablespoons sweet butter
1 tablespoon flour
2 carrots, julienned, cooked al
   dente
4 juniper berries
Pastry for double crust pie

Preheat oven to 450°. Rub ducks generously with thyme, salt and pepper. Place breast up in roasting pan. After 15 minutes, lower heat to 375°: continue roasting until ducks are done, about 1 1/2 hours, pricking occasionally, to release subcutaneous fat. Remove from oven. Pour excess fat from pan. Debone ducks, cut into pieces; set aside. Return bones to pan, cover with water and simmer. Meanwhile, marinate rabbit in vinegar and mustard. Remove, pat dry, and lightly dredge in flour. In cast iron pot, heat oil until hot. Brown rabbit on all sides. Pour in half the wine and enough water to cover meat. Reduce heat, simmer until meat pulls from bone. Debone rabbit, reserving liquid and meat. Add bones to pan of simmering duck bones to make stock. Place large pot over medium heat. Add bacon; cook until most of fat is rendered. Discard fat. Rub pork with garlic, then cube. Brown cubes in oil, and then, about 6-8 minutes before meat is cooked through, add onions and mushrooms, cooking until onion wilts and lightly colors. Deglaze pan with remaining wine. Transfer pork and liquid to bowl. In same pot, make roux with butter and flour. When golden brown, add strained stock from bones to make rich sauce. Stir in all cooked ingredients, their juices, plus carrots and juniper berries. Adjust seasoning; bring just to simmer. Transfer mixture to low-sided casserole and allow to cool. Preheat oven to 375°. Cover casserole with crust, making sure to seal edges well. Cut vents in pastry to allow steam to escape. Bake 35-40 minutes or until top is golden.

Michael Ackerman, The Pantry
Washington Depot

Venison with Rum and Green Peppercorns

Not only does venison taste wonderful, it's high in protein and low in fat. You can use a cut from the leg or the loin. We use the leg, cutting scallopine-type slices.

3 tablespoons butter
Venison slices from leg or loin
Flour
2 teaspoons minced shallots
$1/4$ cup dark rum

$1/2$ cup beef stock
$1/4$ cup heavy cream
2 teaspoons green peppercorns
Salt and ground pepper to taste

Melt butter in heavy skillet. Dip venison slices in flour and sauté to your liking (we recommend medium rare so it doesn't get tough). Remove venison from pan and keep warm. Add shallots to pan. Cook 1 minute. Deglaze pan with rum. Add stock and reduce, 3 minutes. Add cream and reduce, 2 minutes. Add peppercorns, salt and pepper and any juices from venison. Spoon sauce over meat and serve.
4 Servings

**Chefs J. Everin and R. Peters, The Woodland
Lakeville**

Oven Roasted Mushrooms

Roasting brings out the natural, woody, nutty character of wild and cultivated mushrooms. When using fresh wild mushrooms, clean thoroughly.

2 pounds wild or cultivated
   mushrooms, or a mixture
2 tablespoons minced shallots
4 cloves garlic, minced
$1/2$ teaspoon chopped fresh thyme
$1/2$ teaspoon chopped fresh
   rosemary

Salt and pepper to taste
$1/2$ cup white wine
$1/2$ cup olive oil
1 loaf peasant bread

Clean and trim mushrooms, leaving whole. In large bowl, whisk together next 7 ingredients; add mushrooms. Marinate 45 minutes, tossing every 10-15 minutes to coat well. Preheat oven to 500°. Pour mixture into heavy-duty roasting pan and bake, undisturbed, 25 minutes. Dainty mushrooms should roast separately, as they cook faster. Serve as a first course, accompanied by chewy peasant bread for dipping in juices.
6 Servings

**Randy Nichols, Harvest Roasterie
Torrington**

Bacon Baked Rabbit

Like many people in the Litchfield Hills, we hunt and fish for much of our food. We raise organic rabbits, but wild rabbit or squirrel is equally good in this recipe.

1 rabbit, cut in 5-7 pieces
1 cup flour
2 teaspoons fresh black pepper
2 teaspoons garlic powder
1 tablespoon paprika

Salt to taste
1 cup rendered bacon fat
1 cup fine dry bread crumbs
Sage, basil or oregano

Preheat oven to 350°. Mix flour with next 4 ingredients. Lightly coat rabbit in seasoned flour, shaking off excess. Dip pieces in warm bacon fat, allowing excess to drip off. Coat in bread crumbs. Arrange rabbit in baking dish. Bake 30 minutes, then turn pieces and continue baking 30 minutes longer. Rabbit will be brown and crisp when done.
2-4 Servings

Sue and Skip Shook, Running Creek Reservation
Litchfield

Elder Blossom Fritters

Since childhood I have enjoyed picking and eating flowers. These fritters look extremely pretty garnished with maple sugar and additional elder blossoms.

2 cups fine white cornmeal
1 egg, lightly beaten
1 cup water or milk
1 tablespoon maple syrup
$1/4$ cup corn oil for frying

16 elder blossom clusters, washed
    and dried
Maple sugar
Additional blossoms

Prepare light batter, beating together cornmeal, egg, water and maple syrup. Heat oil on griddle and drop batter by large tablespoonfuls onto it, immediately placing 1 blossom cluster in center of each raw fritter and pressing lightly into batter. Fry 3-5 minutes, or until golden. Flip and fry 3 minutes on other side. Drain on brown paper. Serve hot.
8 Servings

Barrie Kavasch
Bridgewater

Blue Ribbon Farm Venison and Wild Rice

You can be as creative with venison as any other meat. Add your own herbs and your favorite Connecticut wine.

3-4 pounds venison stew meat	1¹/₄ teaspoons chopped rosemary
³/₄ cup olive oil	Salt and freshly ground pepper
1¹/₂ teaspoons minced garlic	1 cup dry white wine
¹/₂ tablespoon chopped parsley	Parsley sprigs

Pat venison dry. In large skillet, heat oil and brown meat in batches on all sides, 2-3 minutes. Add garlic and sauté until golden. Stir in parsley, rosemary and season to taste. Remove pan from heat; stir in wine. Cover and cook over low heat 15 minutes. Remove cover and cook until wine evaporates. To serve, pour pan juices over meat and garnish with parsley. Serve with wild rice.
6-8 Servings

Vincent Talarico, Jr., Blue Ribbon Farm
New Milford

Hand-Tapped Maple Syrup Popcorn

We produce our own syrup at Flanders Nature Center.

4 quarts popped corn	2 cups granulated sugar
2 cups pure maple syrup	2 tablespoons butter
1 cup chopped peanuts	1 teaspoon vinegar

In heavy saucepan, combine sugar, syrup and vinegar. Cook over low heat, stirring until sugar dissolves. Cook to 275° on candy thermometer. Remove from heat, add butter and stir until melted. Add peanuts and pour gradually into popcorn, tossing and blending well. Cool.

Flanders Nature Center
Woodbury

Stinging Nettle Soup

A 1969 lecture by Euell Gibbons inspired me to learn about wild foods. The common stinging nettle, which loses its sting when steamed, is one of the earliest and most nutritious greens. Wearing plastic gloves, gather the young tips from fertile areas like old barnyards, from April to June.

1 medium potato, quartered
1 carrot, coarsely chopped
1 onion, coarsely chopped
1 clove garlic
$^1/_2$ pound nettle tops
2 tablespoons flour

2 tablespoons butter
2 cups milk
1 teaspoon dried basil
$^1/_8$ teaspoon grated nutmeg
$^1/_8$ teaspoon dried thyme
Salt and pepper to taste

In saucepan, cover first 4 ingredients with water. Simmer until tender. In separate pan, using metal tongs, arrange nettles. Add 1 cup water and steam until tender. Meanwhile, make a white sauce. Melt butter, whisk in flour and gradually add milk. Stir constantly over low heat until mixture thickens. Purée vegetables and nettles in their cooking water. Pour into soup pot. Add white sauce and seasonings. Reheat gently. Do not boil!
6 Servings

Linda Potter
Washington

Chanterelles on Puff Pastry Squares

In Litchfield County, these prized edibles are found growing under pine or oak trees during July and August. Beginners: always use a dependable field guide or consult an expert before sampling any wild mushrooms! Delicious as an appetizer.

1 medium onion, minced
2 tablespoons sweet butter
1$^1/_2$ cups chanterelles, cleaned
    and sliced

2 ounces dry white wine
2 tablespoons sour cream
4 puff pastry squares or 8 slices
    party rye, toasted

In medium skillet, sauté onion in butter until translucent. Add mushrooms; cook and turn for 5 minutes. Add wine and simmer gently, uncovered, 15 minutes, or until tender. Add sour cream. Serve over puff pastry, or toasted party rye.
4 Servings

Greti Hediger
New Milford

Venison Bourguignonne

In the Litchfield Hills, no freezer is complete without a side of venison. On cold winter evenings my husband loves coming home to a house filled with the delightful aroma of this hearty stew.

3 pounds venison stew meat
Oil or drippings
Salt and pepper
1 large onion, minced
1 cup beef stock
3 tablespoons roux
4 tablespoons tomato paste

Parsley, thyme, bay leaf, celery
   leaves tied in cheesecloth
1 cup Burgundy wine
10 ounces mushrooms, chunked
   and sautéed in butter
24 small whole onions, parboiled

In a skillet, brown meat in oil and season with salt and pepper. With slotted spoon, remove meat from skillet to Dutch oven. To skillet, add onion and cook briefly but do not brown. Add stock, roux and tomato paste. Stirring constantly, bring mixture to boil. When mixture is smooth, add to meat in Dutch oven. Warm slowly, adding Burgundy and herb bouquet. Cover and simmer over low heat until meat is tender, $1^1/2$ hours. Fifteen minutes before serving, add mushrooms and onions and simmer until flavors are blended.
8 Servings

Deborah Swigart
Washington

Fiddleheads and Salsify Roots

As author of "Native Harvests: Recipes & Botanicals of the American Indians", I have long experimented with wild edibles. This is a tasty and exciting vegetable combination.

Salt and freshly ground pepper
2 dozen salsify roots, peeled
$1/2$ cup boiling water

4 dozen ostrich fern fiddleheads
1 tablespoon cider vinegar
1 tablespoon sunflower seed oil

Place salsify roots in medium pot. Cover with water, and steam 10 minutes. Add remaining ingredients. Stir thoroughly; lay fiddleheads on top and simmer, covered, 5 minutes. Serve hot, or marinate further and serve cold.
6-8 Servings

Barrie Kavasch
Bridgewater

Holiday Bourbon-Sauced Pheasant

Traditionally, my husband hunts pheasant Thanksgiving morning with family and friends. (But we always have a back-up turkey!)

1 cup mixed dried fruit, cut up
1 5¹/₂-ounce can apricot nectar
¹/₃ cup bourbon
3¹/₂ cups bread cubes
¹/₂ cup chopped pecans
¹/₂ teaspoon cinnamon

3 tablespoons butter, melted
2 2-pound pheasants
Salt
2 slices bacon, halved crosswise
¹/₄ cup plum jelly

Preheat oven to 350°. In small saucepan, mix dried fruit, nectar and bourbon. Bring to boil, reduce heat, cover and simmer 5 minutes. Remove from heat. Let stand 15 minutes. Drain; reserve liquid. Place bread cubes in baking pan and toast in oven 10-15 minutes until dried. In a large bowl, combine bread, nuts and cinnamon. Drizzle with butter and ¹/₄ cup reserved liquid. Toss until mixed; stir in fruit. Rinse birds and pat dry. Season cavities with salt. Skewer neck skin to back. Spoon stuffing into body cavities (extra stuffing can be baked separately). Tie legs to tails; twist wing tips under. Place birds breast-side up on a rack in shallow roasting pan. Lay bacon over breasts. Roast 1¹/₄-1¹/₂ hours. While bird is roasting, in small saucepan, make sauce by combining jelly with reserved liquid, heating until jelly melts. Fifteen minutes before done, discard bacon, and baste pheasant frequently with plum sauce.
8 Servings

Pat Kennedy Lahoud
Bridgewater

Wild Rice with Real Maple Syrup

As the author of "Native New England Cooking", I often serve this dish to visitors at the Institute for American Indian Studies in Washington, CT. People love it and cannot believe there are only two ingredients. It's best made ahead so the rice can "marinate" in the syrup.

8 ounces wild rice   2 cups real maple syrup

Cook wild rice in 6-8 cups of salted water, covered, for 45-60 minutes. Cool. Fluff with fork. Add syrup, fluff again and let stand. Serve hot or cold. Delicious plain. To enhance, add raisins and a splodge of whipped cream.
6-8 Servings

Dale Carson
Madison

Warm Dandelion and Sorrel Salad with Poached Egg and Bacon

A country version of a bistro classic. The parts can be readied ahead and assembled right before serving. Be sure to use top-of-the-line ingredients — the youngest greens, wonderful bacon from The Egg and I Farm and fresh local eggs.

8 handfuls mixed dandelion and
  sorrel leaves
16 slices thick-cut bacon in
  1" pieces
7 tablespoons olive oil, divided
16 1/4" baguette slices, cut on bias

Garlic clove, peeled
8 very fresh eggs
Splash of white vinegar
4 tablespoons balsamic vinegar
1 tablespoon Dijon mustard
Freshly cracked pepper

Wash and dry greens, removing sorrel ribs if tough. Set aside. Cook bacon until crisp/chewy. Remove bacon, drain. Pour off and save bacon fat. In same skillet, heat 2 tablespoons olive oil. Sauté baguette slices until crisp and golden on both sides. Drain. When cool, rub each side lightly with garlic clove. Fill bowl with very hot tap water, submerge eggs in their shells. (This helps set whites and keeps them from spreading.) In sauté pan, bring more water and white vinegar to boil. Reduce to simmer and carefully crack in eggs. Poach and trim. (Slightly undercook eggs, hold in cold water and rewarm, if serving later.) In bacon skillet, put 5 tablespoons reserved bacon fat, 5 tablespoons olive oil, balsamic vinegar, and mustard. Heat gently, whisking to combine. Toss greens with warm dressing. Divide into 8 rimmed soup plates. Top each salad with 2 croutons, an egg, and bacon chunks. Crack pepper on top.
8 Servings

Judy Perkins
New Milford

More veggies, please

for Woodbury antiquers, concertgoers
on New Milford green---the countryside's
pick of vegetables in season at farm stands
and farmer's markets---beautiful bounty for all.

Ricotta-Stuffed Squash Blossoms

Finally, squash blossoms which don't require batter or frying. Vicki Sebastian's recipe is one of our most requested.

12-15 fresh squash blossoms
1 pound ricotta cheese
1 medium onion, finely chopped
$^1/_2$ cup toasted almonds, finely chopped
$^1/_2$ cup grated fresh Asiago cheese
$^1/_2$ teaspoon ground pepper

1 teaspoon seasoning salt
2 tablespoons finely chopped fresh basil
2 tablespoons finely chopped parsley
2 tablespoons melted butter

Preheat oven to 350°. Mix all filling ingredients together except butter. Stuff squash blossoms carefully; don't overfill. Drizzle melted butter over blossoms and bake 15 minutes.
4 Servings

**Renee Shepherd, Shepherd's Garden Seeds
Torrington**

Off the Cob Corn and Peppers

We get such superb local corn in the summer, we try to be patient and prepare this dish only when it is at its peak.

$^1/_4$ cup cooking oil
1 tablespoon butter
6 ears native corn

1 large red pepper
1 large green pepper
$^1/_2$ cup fresh cilantro, chopped

Husk corn and cut off kernels, placing them in bowl. Do not drain or wash. Cut peppers to medium dice. Heat oil and butter in skillet over medium high heat. Add peppers, stirring until slightly softened. Add corn and continue cooking 5 minutes, stirring and turning once or twice. Reduce heat to medium low, cover, and continue cooking 6-7 minutes, stirring occasionally. Keep sampling corn until done to taste. Just before serving, mix in cilantro. Leftovers can be dressed with oil and vinegar and served over lettuce.
4-6 Servings

**Lans and Debbie Christensen
Washington Depot**

Vegetable Fritters with Tomato Basil Salsa

During the summer we get great fresh vegetables from Gordon Ridgway's farm in Cornwall.

For salsa:
2 ripe tomatoes, chopped
$^1/_4$ cup chopped fresh basil
2 tablespoons olive oil
2 tablespoons red wine vinegar
Salt and fresh pepper
For fritters:
1 small yellow squash, grated
1 small zucchini, grated

1 small carrot, grated
1 small red onion, diced small
1 small red pepper, diced small
1 bunch scallions, diced small
$^1/_2$ cup flour
2 eggs, lightly beaten
1 teaspoon baking soda
Salt and fresh pepper
Oil for frying

Make salsa by combining ingredients. Chill. Mix fritter ingredients in large bowl. Add more flour or egg to adjust batter if necessary. Heat $^1/_4$" oil in skillet until medium hot. Shape 3" fritters and drop into oil. Flatten with spoon if necessary. Cook 2-3 minutes each side. Serve with salsa.

Chefs J. Everin and R. Peters, The Woodland
Lakeville

Celery Root and Parsley Purée

1 large celery root
1 medium potato
Salt, pepper to taste

$^1/_2$ cup heavy cream
3 tablespoons chopped parsley

Peel, and cube celery root and potato. Boil until tender. Put in food processor with seasonings and cream. Purée. Add parsley. Heat and serve.

Audrey Patterson
New Preston

Rosemary Roast Potatoes

Irresistible. There are never any leftovers.

6 large potatoes, scrubbed
$1^1/_2$ tablespoons fresh rosemary
  leaves

1 tablespoon butter or olive oil
Salt
Freshly ground pepper

Preheat oven to 400°. Slice potatoes in half lengthwise. Place halves, cut side down, on board. Holding knife on slant, cut each half into 4 or 6 wedges, lengthwise. Place in roasting pan coated with non-stick cooking spray. Dot with butter, sprinkle with rosemary and season to taste. Roast 45-60 minutes until crispy and browned, turning occasionally. Serve immediately.
4 Servings

Tom Rush
New Milford

Creamy Crunchy Vegetable Stuffing

This is a terrific side dish with grilled sea bass or shrimp.

3 medium zucchini, peeled and
   sliced
2 small onions, sliced
2 carrots, shredded
1 can water chestnuts drained and
   diced
1 cup cabbage, shredded

2 cups vegetable stock or bouillon,
   divided
2 tablespoons celery seed
1 teaspoon black pepper
2 cups coarse bread crumbs
1 cup plain yoghurt or sour cream

Preheat oven to 350°. Sauté squash, onions, carrots, water chestnuts, and cabbage in $1/2$ cup of vegetable stock. Keep vegetables on crisp side. Add celery seed and black pepper. Mix together bread crumbs and remaining $1^1/2$ cups vegetable stock. Put $3/4$ of this mixture in bottom of $2^1/2$ quart casserole dish. Place sautéed vegetable mixture on top, spread yoghurt or sour cream on top of mixture. Add rest of bread crumbs. Bake 30 minutes.

Peter Dubos
Danbury

Baby Limas in Sour Cream Sauce

1 pound dried baby lima beans
$1/4$ cup butter, melted
$1/4$ cup light brown sugar
$1/4$ cup molasses

2 tablespoons prepared honey
   mustard
1 teaspoon salt
1 cup sour cream

Soak beans overnight. Drain. Cover with fresh water and cook until tender. Do not overcook. Drain beans thoroughly. Preheat oven to 350°. In separate bowl, combine and mix remaining ingredients thoroughly. Combine with beans. Butter oven-proof baking dish and pour in bean mixture. Bake 40-45 minutes, until hot.

Karen Miles
Marbledale

Late Summer Garden Ratatouille

In 1986, Buck's Rock Camp hired a young chef from Lyon, France, Eric Barbecot. He was a most competent, charming and creative fellow, who enjoyed creating recipes for the vegetarians in our midst.

2 large eggplant
4 medium zucchinis
1 teaspoon salt
4 tablespoons olive oil
2 medium onions
2 green peppers

Garlic, chopped
6 tomatoes, coarsely sliced
Salt, pepper to taste
3 tablespoons chopped parsley
Grated cheese

Slice eggplant and zucchini in $^3/_8$" thick lengthwise strips. Sprinkle with salt and let stand 30 minutes; rinse and dry. Sauté eggplant and zucchini slices in olive oil until brown on both sides, set aside. Cook onions and peppers until soft. Add garlic and tomatoes. Cover and cook 15 minutes. Add salt, pepper, and parsley. In $1^1/_2$ quart casserole, layer, starting with $^1/_3$ of the tomato sauce. Follow with layer of eggplant, then layer of zucchini. Add another layer of tomato sauce. Repeat eggplant and zucchini. Top off with remaining tomato sauce. Cover and bake 10 minutes. Uncover, baste. Bake 15 more minutes. Cut in wedges, top with grated cheese.
4-6 Servings

Roberta Berger
New Milford

Spinach Japanese Style

This spinach may also be shaped into tiny balls to garnish a cold meat platter or appetizer tray.

1 pound fresh spinach, washed
    and trimmed or 2 packages
    frozen, chopped
$^1/_4$ cup sesame seeds

$^1/_4$ cup soy sauce
2 tablespoons sugar or less, to
    taste

In large pot, steam spinach until wilted. Drain, cool, squeeze dry and chop. If frozen spinach is used, thaw and squeeze out excess moisture. In skillet, over medium high heat, toast sesame seeds. Pulverize in mortar and pestle, or in blender. Combine spinach with sesame, soy sauce and sugar to taste. Serve chilled or at room temperature.
4-6 Servings

Maggie Smith
Kent

Eggplant à la Basque

Herbs are a passion of mine, which is why I love this recipe. I often feature it in box lunches. It keeps well and is a big hit every time.

2 medium eggplant, unpeeled, cut
   in 1/2" slices
3 tablespoons olive or vegetable
   oil
3 onions, finely sliced
1 or 2 cloves garlic, minced
4 tomatoes, peeled and chopped
1 tablespoon fresh thyme,
   chopped

2-3 tablespoons fresh basil,
   chopped
Salt and pepper
1 cup feta cheese, crumbled
2 tablespoons chopped parsley,
   divided

Preheat oven to 350°. Brown eggplant in oil, adding more oil as needed. Place in greased 8"x8" baking dish. Sauté onions and garlic in pan. Add tomatoes, herbs, salt and pepper to taste. Simmer until thick. Add feta cheese. Spoon mixture over eggplant, sprinkle with 1 tablespoon parsley. Bake, uncovered, 45 minutes or until set and brown. Garnish with remaining parsley. Serve hot or cold.
4-6 Servings

Georgianna Middlebrook
Washington

Roast Potato Fans with Chives

Crispy, golden and impressive. Expect diners to ignore everything else on the plate.

6 large baking potatoes
1/4 cup butter, melted
1/2 teaspoon salt
4 tablespoons chopped fresh
   chives

1/2 cup grated cheese
3 tablespoons bread crumbs

Preheat oven to 350°. Peel potatoes and place in cold water until ready to use. Dry and cut thin slice off long side of each potato so it sits flat. With sharp knife, cut vertical slits from the top almost to bottom of each potato, being careful not to cut through. Dip cut potatoes in melted butter and sprinkle with salt. Bake on foil-lined baking sheet for 1 1/2 hours, basting with remaining butter. Potatoes will turn golden brown and the slits will open in accordion fashion. In the last 15 minutes, combine chives, cheese and bread crumbs and stuff into potato slits.
6 Servings

Renee Shepherd, Shepherd's Garden Seeds
Torrington

Savory Asparagus Timbales

1 sprig fresh thyme leaves
2 sprigs fresh rosemary leaves
2 cloves garlic, minced
1 tablespoon Dijon mustard
1 teaspoon ground cumin
3 cups milk

4 whole eggs plus 2 egg yolks
1 pound asparagus, cut into
    1" slices
Salt and pepper to taste
$1/4$ cup vegetable oil

Preheat oven to 325°. In 2 quart saucepan, combine herbs, garlic, mustard, cumin and milk, bring to boil and take off heat. In bowl, beat eggs with yolks, add milk mixture, stir in asparagus, season with salt and pepper. Lightly oil custard cups; fill $3/4$" full with custard mix; place cups in roasting pan. Pour enough boiling water in pan to come halfway up sides of cups. Bake in center of oven 1 hour until center of custard is almost firm to touch. Remove from water bath. Let set 3 minutes. To unmold, run knife around sides and quickly turn onto plate.
8 Servings

Carole Peck, Carole Peck Catering
New Preston

Apricot-Glazed Carrots

Even carrot-haters like these. An easy recipe for everyday, but special enough for entertaining. Good with poultry or pork.

2 pounds carrots, scraped and cut
    on diagonal
3 tablespoons butter or margarine
$1/3$ cup apricot preserves
$1/4$ teaspoon ground nutmeg

$1/4$ teaspoon salt
$1/2$-1 teaspoon freshly grated
    orange peel
2 teaspoons fresh lemon juice
Parsley for garnish

Cook carrots in salted water until just tender, about 20 minutes. Drain. Melt butter and stir in preserves until blended. Add nutmeg, salt, orange peel and lemon juice. Toss carrots with apricot mixture until well coated. Garnish with parsley and serve at once.
4-6 Servings

Nancy Fyfield
New Milford

Ginger Baked Squash

The New Milford Farmers' Market inspired this dish, when I spotted a heap of baby squash huddled like fat birds in a wooden flat. It's especially good with wild duck or goose.

2-3 medium onions, finely diced
2-3 tablespoons fresh ginger root, peeled and grated
Butter or olive oil
2 baked baby hubbard squash or steamed butternut squash
2 eggs, beaten

Dash of milk or cream
Handful of parsley, finely chopped
1 tablespoon grated lemon rind
Freshly ground black pepper to taste

Preheat oven to 350°. Gently sauté onions and grated ginger in butter until onions are soft and translucent. Peel squash when cool enough to handle, mash in large mixing bowl. Add eggs, ginger, onion mixture, milk, extra butter if you wish, parsley, lemon rind and pepper. Mix and turn into buttered 2 quart baking dish. Bake, covered, 45 minutes, uncover to brown another 15 minutes.

Karen Bussolini
South Kent

Sweet Yellow Pepper Purée

I like this warm in the winter or cold with fish or steak in the summer. It's very pretty in a cut glass bowl, garnished with basil leaves.

$1/4$ cup olive oil
6 large sweet yellow peppers
1 large yellow onion, chopped
2 cloves garlic, minced

2 tablespoons chopped fresh basil
Salt and freshly ground pepper to taste

Core, seed, and cut peppers into $1/4$" dice. Heat oil in medium-sized skillet over high heat. Add yellow peppers, onion and garlic. Sauté 10 minutes. Reduce heat to low, cover pan and simmer 30 minutes. Transfer pepper mixture to food processor. Add basil, salt and pepper to taste. Process until smooth. Remove to saucepan and heat to boiling. Cook, uncovered, over medium high heat, stirring frequently, until reduced and slightly thickened, 5-10 minutes.
6 Servings

Christine Ford

Leeks Au Gratin

Being an avid gardener, I love recipes that do justice to my hard work. I make these often and there are never any leftovers.

4 medium leeks including tender
    tops, cut in $^1/_2$" pieces
1 tablespoon margarine
1 tablespoon plus 1 teaspoon flour
$^1/_4$ teaspoon salt
Freshly ground pepper to taste

$^2/_3$ cup skim milk
$^1/_2$ cup shredded Gruyère cheese
For topping:
2 tablespoons bread crumbs
1 teaspoon melted margarine

Preheat oven to 325°. Heat 1" of water to boiling. Add leeks. Cover and cook over medium heat 5 minutes or until crisp/tender. Prepare topping and put aside. Spray shallow 1 quart casserole with non-stick cooking spray. Heat margarine in 2 quart saucepan over low heat. Stir in flour, salt and pepper, stirring constantly until margarine is absorbed; remove from heat. Gradually stir in milk. Heat to boiling, stirring constantly. Boil and stir 1 minute. Stir in cheese until melted. Stir in leeks. Pour into casserole. Mix bread crumbs and margarine for topping and sprinkle on top. Bake, uncovered, 25 minutes or until heated through.
4 Servings

Dolores Hennessy
New Milford

Carrots Fenugreek

This dish is very pretty and has a wonderful mapley flavor. We serve it often at Catnip Acres with fish or chicken.

2 cups carrots, scraped
3 tablespoons frozen orange juice
    concentrate, undiluted
$^1/_2$ cup water
1 teaspoon fenugreek seed
1 tablespoon brown sugar

Salt to taste
2 tablespoons butter
$^3/_4$ cup Italian flavored bread
    crumbs
$^1/_3$ cup grated Parmesan cheese

Preheat oven to 350°. Cut carrots into "lunchbox" sized sticks. Steam carrots until almost tender, then transfer into greased casserole. Mix orange juice concentrate, water, fenugreek seed, sugar and salt. Pour over carrots. Melt butter, stir in bread crumbs. Sprinkle carrots with crumbs, then with Parmesan. Bake 20-30 minutes until bubbly and lightly browned.
4 Servings

Ms. Gene Banks, Catnip Acres Herb Nursery
Oxford

Garden Green and Gold

This is a pretty dish and it's also practical when your squash crop is a bit too successful.

3 medium zucchini
3 medium yellow squash
Olive oil for frying
$^1/_2$ cup whole basil leaves
1 tablespoon garlic oil
2-3 shallots, minced

Salt and freshly ground pepper
3 tablespoons sundried tomatoes, chopped
3 tablespoons good red wine vinegar

Wash and trim squash; cut in $^1/_4$" slices. Heat $^1/_4$" olive oil in large heavy skillet. Sauté squash a few at a time, until lightly browned on both sides. Remove with slotted spoon (do not drain) to 12"-14" serving dish. Alternating yellow and green, slightly overlap slices in concentric circles in a single layer. Tuck in basil leaves. Sprinkle with garlic oil, shallots, salt, pepper, tomatoes and vinegar. Let stand at least 1 hour. Serve at room temperature.
6-8 Servings

Florence and Wendell Minor
Washington

Summer Squash Delight

This sunshiny casserole is equally good as a side dish or vegetarian entrée.

2 pounds yellow squash, coarsely chopped
1 medium onion, coarsely chopped
2 eggs, beaten
$^1/_3$ cup evaporated milk or half and half

2 tablespoons butter
$1^3/_4$ cups grated Cheddar cheese, divided
Salt, pepper, garlic to taste
$^1/_2$ cup buttered cracker crumbs

Preheat oven to 350°. Cook squash and onion together in small amount of water. Drain. Add eggs, milk or cream, butter, $1^1/_2$ cups of the cheese and seasonings. Turn into greased $1^1/_2$ quart casserole; spread crumbs and remaining cheese on top. Bake 30 minutes, uncovered.
6 Servings

Richard Widmark
Roxbury

Autumn Harvest Medley

This dish is a nice accompaniment to home-smoked roast turkey or ham. If you don't own a smoker, there are several good smokehouses in Litchfield County.

1 medium-sized butternut squash
2 small or 1 large acorn squash
2 small sweet potatoes, baked
3 firm, tart red apples (such as
    Rome, Cortland)
3 tablespoons sweet butter, melted
    and divided

Salt to taste
$^1/_4$ cup maple syrup
Fresh grated nutmeg
2 teaspoons fresh grated orange
    rind, optional

Halve and seed squash and place on steamer rack in large kettle. Steam until fork tender. Do not overcook. Meanwhile, peel, core and halve apples. Steam in separate pot, until soft. When cool enough to handle, scoop squash pulp into large mixing bowl. Halve sweet potatoes and scoop out into bowl, along with steamed apples. Using potato masher, combine ingredients until fairly smooth, but still retaining some texture. Stir in 2 tablespoons butter, maple syrup and salt to taste. Turn into shallow, buttered, 2 quart baking dish. Dust with nutmeg and orange rind, if desired. Just before serving, brush remaining butter over surface and run under a preheated broiler until lightly browned.
6-8 Servings

William Irving
South Kent

Lentil and Sweet Potato Stew

Nutritious and delicious, this is best made a day or two ahead. You can add meat but it's a great non-meat entrée.

$^1/_4$ cup olive oil
1 large onion, chopped
3 cloves garlic, chopped
$1^1/_2$ cups ham or turkey sausage,
    optional
2 tablespoons "Vegit" (dry herbs)
3 medium sweet potatoes or
    yams, peeled and cubed

4 ounces currants
6 cups chicken broth
1 bay leaf
Pepper to taste
1 cup dry lentils

In a large pot, sauté onion and garlic in oil over medium heat. Add meat if using. Add remaining ingredients and simmer, covered, for approximately $1^1/_2$ hours.
6 Servings

Karin Rost
Sharon

The Otis Express Tortilla

This is a great light snack or lunch, depending on how many toppings you add. All toppings are grown on our farm, or can be found seasonally throughout New England.

Corn or flour tortilla
Lemon flavored salt
Monterey Jack, Cheddar or any
    goat cheese, grated
Basil

Garlic
Eggplant, broccoli, kale, onions,
    chard, tomatoes, peppers
Oregano

Preheat oven to 350°. Lay out tortilla and sprinkle with lemon flavored salt. Spread desired cheeses on tortilla; add garlic and basil. Add toppings (kale and chard are best in colder months due to local availability). Top with more cheese and oregano. Bake for 5-8 minutes or until tortilla is crisp.

Dan Horan, Waldingfield Farm
Washington

Incredibly Easy Eggplant Stew

Make this days ahead. It travels beautifully and reheats well. It's a ski trip stand-by for our family.

$1^1/_2$ -2 pounds eggplant, cut in 2"
    cubes
1 teaspoon salt, or to taste
2 large onions, peeled and sliced
$1/_2$ cup olive oil
$1/_2$ (or more) zucchini, sliced

1 cup chick peas, cooked
2 cups canned tomatoes, drained
    with juice reserved
3 cloves garlic, minced
$1^1/_2$ teaspoons basil
$1/_3$ cup olive oil

Preheat oven to 400°. Sauté eggplant and onions in olive oil until soft, stirring occasionally, 10 minutes. Add zucchini and chick peas (drained, if canned). Sauté five more minutes. Make sauce: cook together for 10 minutes, drained tomatoes, plus 1 cup reserved juice, garlic, basil and olive oil. Put eggplant mixture in a 6"x11"x3" roasting pan and pour on sauce. Bake 45 minutes.
8 Servings

Anne Perry Todd, Party Resources
Kent

Hearty Vegetable Chili

This is a great chili for parties. It's extremely healthy but so robust it satisfies even the most obdurate meat-eater. Use an assortment of beans such as kidney, cannellini, black, white, pink, or pinto.

2 tablespoons olive oil
3 large onions, chopped
$^1/_3$ cup chopped garlic
2 jalapeño chilies, minced with seeds
2 28-ounce cans plum tomatoes, drained, diced (reserve juice)

$^1/_2$ cup tomato paste
2 green bell peppers, chopped
2 large carrots, chopped
1 tablespoon ground cumin
$^3/_4$ teaspoon salt
$^1/_2$ teaspoon cayenne pepper
4 15-ounce cans beans, drained

Heat olive oil. Sauté onions, garlic, and chilies until onions are translucent. Add tomatoes with cup of reserved juice and remaining ingredients. Simmer 20 minutes, stirring frequently. Thin with additional tomato juice if too thick.
8 Servings

Judith Mulvey
Bridgewater

Basil Cilantro Corn Cakes

3 cups fresh corn kernels
1 cup milk
$^2/_3$ cup flour
$^2/_3$ cup cornmeal
1 teaspoon baking powder
4 eggs
4 egg yolks
8 tablespoons butter, melted
$^1/_2$ cup cilantro, finely chopped

$^1/_2$ cup basil, finely chopped
1 teaspoon salt
1 teaspoon freshly ground pepper
4-5 tablespoons olive oil, or more if needed
For garnish:
1 cup crème fraîche
Basil and cilantro

Process corn and milk until chunky and creamy; pour into bowl. Add flour, cornmeal and baking powder; mix well. In another mixing bowl, beat together eggs, egg yolks and butter until smooth and frothy. Add this mixture to the corn mixture and combine well. Add herbs, salt and pepper. Heat oil in skillet. For each small cake, ladle $1^1/_2$ ounces of batter into hot oil. Fry 2 minutes per side, until nicely browned and cooked through. To serve: place 4-6 cakes on each plate. Garnish with a dollop of crème fraîche, basil and cilantro.
Yield: 24 cakes

James O'Shea, West Street Grill
Litchfield

Vegetarian "Meatballs" in Yoghurt Sauce

Meat-eaters will never miss the meat in this dish!

3 cakes tofu
3 tablespoons vegetable oil
2 large onions, diced
4 cloves garlic, minced
3 medium carrots, grated
2 eggs, beaten
1^1/$_4$ cups bread crumbs
1 cup almonds, lightly toasted and
   ground
2 tablespoons Dijon mustard
^{1}/$_4$ cup tamari
1 tablespoon sesame oil

1 teaspoon ground fennel
^{1}/$_2$ teaspoon ground caraway
   seeds
2 teaspoons basil
^{1}/$_4$ cup chopped fresh parsley
For sauce:
4 eggs, beaten
2 cups plain yoghurt
2 teaspoons ground caraway
   seeds
1 tablespoon dill

Place tofu between two hand towels and weigh down with something heavy. After 15 minutes towels will absorb most of moisture and tofu will be ready to use. Preheat oven to 350°. Heat oil; sauté onion, garlic and carrots until onions are translucent. Set aside. Mix together next 10 ingredients. Crumble pressed tofu into mixture, then add sautéed vegetables and mix well. Form into 2" balls. Place on oiled baking sheet. Bake 25-30 minutes until browned. Meanwhile, make sauce by combining eggs, yoghurt, caraway seeds and dill in saucepan. Heat gently, stirring constantly until thickened. Serve over meatballs.
Yield: 24 meatballs

James Taylor
Washington

Oven Roasted Beets

Roasting beets intensifies their natural flavor so none of the garden goodness is lost. Using the oven is also easier and a lot less messy than boiling or steaming.

Fresh beets

Preheat oven to 400°. Trim greens from beets (they're great in salad) and scrub beets well. Wrap beets individually in foil and roast for one hour or until just tender. Poke through with a skewer to check for doneness. When cool enough to handle, slip off peels and cut as desired.

Arthur Schwartz
Cornwall

Summer Lasagna with Zucchini "Noodles"

2 large zucchini
1/2 pound ground beef
1 clove garlic, minced
1/2 teaspoon salt
1 32-ounce jar spaghetti sauce
1 6-ounce can tomato paste

2 cups low-fat cottage cheese
1/2 cup grated Parmesan cheese
2 tablespoons chopped parsley
2 eggs, lightly beaten
1 pound mozzarella cheese,
   shredded

Slice zucchini lengthwise in 1/4" slices. Parboil and drain. Pat dry. Brown meat with garlic and salt. Drain off fat. Stir in spaghetti sauce and tomato paste and set aside. Mix cottage cheese, Parmesan, parsley and eggs. Preheat oven to 350°. Arrange a layer of zucchini in 13"x9"x2" baking pan. Spread with layer of cheese mixture, layer of meat sauce and layer of mozzarella. Continue layers, saving enough meat sauce and mozzarella for the top. Bake until bubbly (approximately 30 minutes). Let stand 10 minutes before cutting.
8-10 Servings

Bobbie Burnett
South Kent

Sidekicks

the relishes, preserves, jams,
chutneys and other condiments
you make yourself that
put your signature on every meal.

Peach Chutney Millstone Farm

This is always good to have on hand to enhance a curry, and it's especially easy when you have your own peach orchard! Besides, as my neighbor Brother Aelred Seton-Shanley says, "Blessed are the Peach-Makers."

1 medium onion, chopped finely
1 clove garlic, chopped finely
1 cup raisins
$2^1/_2$ quarts cut up peaches
1 cup crystallized ginger

2 tablespoons chili powder
2 tablespoons mustard seeds
1 tablespoon salt
1 quart vinegar
$2^1/_2$ cups light brown sugar

Combine all ingredients. Bring to boil. Stir until sugar dissolves. Simmer uncovered 1 hour or more until thick and deep brown. Seal in Ball jars.

Joan Larned, Millstone Farm
Kent

Best of Show Strawberry Jam

My dad and I pick strawberries every year at Starbuck Farm in Washington. The owner's son is a junior counselor at The Pratt Center camp. Last year my mom made the strawberries into a jam that won best of show at the Bridgewater Fair.

1 small orange, unpeeled,
    quartered and seeded
1 small lemon, unpeeled,
    quartered and seeded
3 pints strawberries, washed and
    hulled
2 8-ounce cans crushed
    pineapple, drained

1 cup golden raisins
8 cups sugar
Cinnamon stick
$^1/_4$ teaspoon freshly ground
    nutmeg
$^1/_4$ teaspoon ground allspice

Place orange and lemon in food processor fitted with metal blade and process until coarsely chopped. Add the berries; process until coarsely chopped. Put mixture in heavy saucepan; add remaining 6 ingredients. Bring mixture to simmer over medium heat, stirring frequently. Reduce heat; simmer 20-25 minutes. Remove cinnamon stick. Spoon into sterilized jars. Process according to manufacturer's directions. Store jars in cool, dark place.
Yield: 8 half-pints

Daren Daniels
New Milford

Indonesian Pickles

Turmeric adds flavor and a bright yellow color to these lightly spiced sweet and sour pickles. Originally part of a multi-dish Indonesian "rijstafel", these are equally at home at a Fourth of July barbecue.

3-4 large, firm cucumbers
2 teaspoons turmeric
3 teaspoons salt
³/₄ cup granulated sugar
³/₄ cup white vinegar
1 cup water
8 whole cloves

1 medium yellow onion, finely
  chopped
¹/₂-1 teaspoon chopped fresh
  ginger root
16 drops Chinese hot chili oil,
  optional

Wash and sterilize one quart-sized mason jar and lid. Peel cucumbers, slice lengthwise, remove core and seeds, then slice in long diagonal slices between ¹/₄" and ¹/₂" thick. Stand slices lengthwise in jar and set aside while you prepare sauce. In a medium sized, non-reactive saucepan, combine all remaining ingredients. Bring to boil; reduce heat to medium and cook 8-10 minutes. Pour hot sauce over cucumbers in jar and seal. Cool, then refrigerate until ready to serve. (No need to process filled jar; it keeps fresh in refrigerator at least 2 weeks.)
Yield: 1 quart

Susan G. Purdy
Roxbury

Janice's Pickled Basil Beans

These crispy basil-scented beans are a fine starter, pleasing appetites without spoiling them. Of course, they are best when grown from Shepherd's Garden Seeds.

3-4 pounds fresh-picked green
  snap beans, rinsed
5 cups mild white vinegar
5 cups water
1 tablespoon sugar

¹/₄ cup pickling salt
For each jar:
4 peppercorns
2 garlic cloves, peeled
4-6 large basil leaves

Wash quart or pint jars with hot soapy water and rinse, or run through dishwasher. Trim ends of beans. Bring vinegar, water, sugar and salt to boil. In bottom of each jar, put peppercorns, garlic cloves and basil leaves, then pack jars with beans, leaving ¹/₂" headspace. Fill jars with hot brine, leaving ¹/₂". Wipe jar rims and seal. Process 15 minutes in boiling water bath (20 minutes for quarts). Wait about 4 weeks before opening to let flavors blend and deepen.
Yield: 8 pints or 4 quarts

Renee Shepherd, Shepherd's Garden Seeds
Torrington

Crunchy Cucumber Pickles

This is a great way to use cucumbers and herbs when you have a bountiful harvest. It's fast, and perfect for summertime picnics. Make these ahead so the flavors have time to bloom; they keep for several months in the refrigerator.

3 large cucumbers

1 large onion

$^1/_2$ cup tarragon vinegar

1 teaspoon chopped parsley

1 teaspoon chopped dill weed

$^1/_4$ teaspoon black pepper

1 scant tablespoon salt

1 tablespoon sugar

Slice unpeeled cucumbers $^1/_8$" thick (about 3 cups). Slice onion into thin rings. Combine vinegar, parsley, dill weed, pepper, salt and sugar. Mix well. Pour over cucumbers and onions in glass bowl. Toss well. Store in an airtight glass container. Refrigerate.

Jane Uzwiak
New Milford

Champagne Vinaigrette

1 egg yolk

1 teaspoon whole grain mustard

1 cup salad oil

$^1/_4$ cup red wine vinegar

$^1/_2$ teaspoon salt

Freshly ground black pepper

$^1/_4$-$^1/_2$ cup Champagne

Mix egg yolk and mustard with a few drops of vinegar. Whisk in salad oil slowly alternating with a few drops of vinegar. Whisk in rest of ingredients.

Maison LeBlanc
New Milford

Sweet and Hot Mustard

Perfect for sandwiches and roasts, house presents and holiday gifts.

1 cup mustard .

1 cup vinegar, cider or white

1 cup sugar

2 eggs, well beaten

1 teaspoon salt

1 teaspoon dill

Mix mustard and vinegar, cover; leave for 8 hours or overnight at room temperature. Cook with other ingredients in double boiler; stir until slightly thickened. Recipe can be doubled.
Yield: 1 pint

Jolene Mullen
New Milford

Homemade Pickled Beets

These beets are great, especially when the beets, peppers and onions are from your backyard garden.

2 quarts (8 cups) diced cooked
   beets
3 small onions, sliced
3 green peppers, sliced

1 6-ounce jar horseradish
2 cups cider vinegar
3 cups sugar
3 teaspoons salt

Heat vinegar and dissolve sugar and salt in it. Add horseradish and bring to boil. Add onions, peppers, beets and simmer 20 minutes. Place in sterilized jars. Vacuum seal for 12 minutes or just put in refrigerator.

Amelia Jimenez
Bridgewater

Good Thyme Farm Classic Pesto

Homemade pesto is a kitchen staple for us. We not only add it to minestrone, hot pasta and salad dressing, we stuff it into mushrooms and roll it inside chicken cutlets.

4 cups fresh basil leaves
$^1/_2$ cup fresh parsley leaves
3 + cloves garlic
$^1/_2$ cup pine nuts

1 teaspoon salt
$^1/_2$-1 cup olive oil
$^1/_2$ cup freshly grated Parmesan
   cheese

Combine basil, parsley, garlic, pine nuts, salt and $^1/_2$ cup oil in food processor. Process, adding more oil if necessary, until smooth paste is formed. Stir in cheese.
Yield: 20 ounces

Eileen Mendyka, Good Thyme Farm
Bethlehem

Beet Jelly

This is a fourth generation family recipe. Serve with chicken, turkey or ham.

4 cups cooked beets
4 cups sugar
1 cup vinegar

1 teaspoon salt
1 bottle Certo

Cook beets with skin on. Cool, remove skins and mash. Combine sugar, vinegar and salt. Bring to boil and cook 10 minutes. Add beets and Certo. Cook 5 more minutes. Put into 4 small sterilized jars.
Yield: 4 half-pints

Manon Boucher

Jim's Venison Sauce

An old family favorite. Delicious with roast venison or other game.

1 cup homemade tomato
    preserves
2 tablespoons lemon juice
2 tablespoons freshly grated
    orange rind

2 ounces port wine
1 tablespoon dry mustard, or to
    taste
1 tablespoon cornstarch
1 cup cold water

Combine first 5 ingredients in small, heavy saucepan. Bring to a boil; reduce heat and simmer gently 5-10 minutes. It can be done ahead to this point, allowing flavors to marry. Just before serving, combine cornstarch and water in a measuring cup. Stir into preserve mixture and heat to boiling, stirring constantly. Simmer until sauce is no longer cloudy, 1-2 minutes.
Yield: $1^1/_2$-2 cups

Walter Irving
South Kent

Ellsworth Hill Farm Apple Chutney

This sweet and spicy chutney is delicious with lamb or poultry. Of course it's at its absolute best when made with our Sharon apples! It will keep for several months in the refrigerator if tightly covered.

12 tart apples, peeled, cored and
    sliced
2 large green peppers, finely
    chopped
2 large onions, finely chopped
1 3-ounce can green chili peppers,
    seeded and finely chopped
3 garlic cloves, minced
$1/_2$ cup fresh ginger, peeled and
    minced

Zest and juice from one orange
2 teaspoons salt
$1/_2$ teaspoon cayenne
$3^1/_2$ cups brown sugar
2 cups cider vinegar
$1^1/_2$ cups dried currants
1 cup walnuts, chopped

Put apples in slightly salted water to prevent discoloring while preparing other ingredients. Drain apples. Mix with remaining ingredients in large pot. Cook, uncovered, over low heat, stirring frequently until thick, about 3 hours.
Yield: 8 cups

Jean Vitalis, Ellsworth Hill Farm
Sharon

Roasted Garlic Confit

This makes a very pretty garnish on a meat platter or individual dinner plates. It also works well as a condiment or appetizer. Serve ¹/₂ bulb with crusty bread and a butter knife or demitasse spoon for spreading.

6 large garlic bulbs, halved   1 cup extra virgin olive oil

Preheat oven to 300°. Spread garlic halves face down on cookie sheet. Drizzle with oil. Bake 30-40 minutes. Transfer with oil, into shallow container, keeping garlic cloves in their shells. Serve as desired.
12 servings

Toni Ripinsky and Chris Zaima, Thé Café
New Preston

Ruby Raspberry Jam

Here's a simple, delicious solution for an over-abundant raspberry crop!

2 quarts raspberries (8 cups)   Grated lemon rind to taste
2¹/₂ cups sugar

Preheat oven to 350°. Heat sugar in oven 10 minutes. Meanwhile, pick over berries. Place berries in pan with sugar and mash down with potato masher. Add lemon rind and return to oven. Cook 30-40 minutes, until bubbly around edges, stirring occasionally. Cool at room temperature overnight. Jam will thicken as it stands. Put into sterilized ¹/₂ pint jars and process in boiling water bath.
Yield: 4-5 half-pints

Ayliffe Borie
New Milford

Fruits of your labour

mouth-watering fruit and berry desserts
to assemble from your pick of New Preston's orchards
and farms---to savour at home, or perhaps
at a picnic at Lime Rock.

Averill Farm Apple Pie

This recipe uses lots of apples and makes a full thick pie. For the best flavor combine several varieties of apples.

Pastry for double crust 10" deep dish pie	1 teaspoon cinnamon
	3 tablespoons flour
12 cups apples, peeled, cored and sliced	1 tablespoon lemon juice
	1 teaspoon grated lemon peel
1 cup light brown sugar	2 tablespoons butter

Fill 3 quart saucepan with apple slices. Add $^1/_4$ cup water, cook until bubbly and nearly tender, about 10 minutes. Remove pan from heat, cool slightly. Preheat oven to 425°. Mix remaining ingredients except butter and toss gently with apple slices. Put all in pastry lined, 10" deep dish pie pan. Dot with butter. Cover with top crust. Flute edges, seal and slit top. Bake 45 minutes or until light brown.

Jean Averill, Averill Farm
Washington Depot

Marzipan Fruit Tart with Currant Glaze

This elegant tart is simply Swedish almond paste in a shortbread crust topped with fresh fruit of the season. May prepare crust and filling ahead and top with fruit and glaze several hours before serving.

For crust:	For filling:
$1^1/_4$ cups flour	$1^1/_2$ cups almonds
1 stick butter	$^1/_2$ cup confectioners' sugar
1 egg yolk	2 large egg whites
3 tablespoons sugar	Seasonal fruit
	$^1/_2$ cup currant jelly

Preheat oven to 350°. Make crust. Combine all ingredients in food processor. Add cold water if necessary until dough forms a ball. Roll out or press with fingers into 9" fluted tart pan with removable bottom. Bake 15 minutes or until edges are golden. Make filling. Combine almonds, sugar, and egg whites in food processor. Add more almonds for firmer consistency. Spread in baked tart crust. Top decoratively with fruit. Spread warm currant jelly over fruit just before serving.
8 Servings

Anne Kimball
Washington

Cream Cheese Apple Torte

For crust:
1/2 cup margarine
1/3 cup sugar
1/4 teaspoon vanilla
1 cup flour
For filling:
1 8-ounce package cream cheese,
    softened
1/4 cup sugar

1 egg
1/2 teaspoon vanilla
For topping:
1/4 cup sugar
1/2 teaspoon cinnamon
3 cups apples, peeled, sliced
1/3 cup chopped walnuts or 1/3
    cup sliced almonds.

Preheat oven to 450°. Cream margarine, sugar, vanilla. Blend in flour. Spread dough mixture over bottom and about 1 1/2" up sides of 9" springform pan. Mix cream cheese and sugar until smooth. Add egg and vanilla. Mix thoroughly. Pour into pastry lined pan. Mix sugar with cinnamon and toss apples into mixture. Arrange sliced apples over cream layer. Sprinkle with nuts. Bake for 10 minutes. Reduce temperature to 400° and continue baking for 25 minutes. Loosen torte from rim of pan. Cool before removing the rim.

Viola Dubos
Danbury

Deep-Dish Gooseberry Pie

An excellent dessert for Thanksgiving or after any heavy, winter meal. Serve warm with cream or custard sauce.

1 32-ounce can or jar gooseberries
1/3 cup flour
Dash of salt
1 cup sugar
2 tablespoons butter

2 tablespoons brandy
1 tablespoon grated lemon peel
Rich pastry dough
Sugar

Preheat oven to 425°. Drain gooseberries, reserving one cup juice. Combine flour, salt, sugar, and juice in saucepan. Bring to boil, stirring constantly. Reduce heat, and cook, stirring, for 5 minutes. Add butter, brandy, and peel, stirring until well-blended. Grease 9" soufflé dish, fill with gooseberries. Pour mixture over berries. Cover with pastry dough and sprinkle crust with sugar. Bake 30-40 minutes or until dough turns golden brown.
8 Servings

The Reverend Roger B. White
Kent

Fresh Peach Pie in Coconut Almond Crust

For crust:
1 cup blanched almonds
1 cup moist style flaked coconut
$^1/_4$ cup sugar
$^1/_4$ cup butter
For filling:
1 cup sour cream
Dash salt

6 tablespoons confectioners'
   sugar, divided
1 teaspoon orange juice
1 teaspoon shredded orange rind
1 teaspoon vanilla
3 cups fresh peaches, peeled and
   sliced
1 cup whipping cream

Preheat oven to 350°. For crust, grind almonds medium fine and mix with coconut. Work in sugar and butter. Press into bottom and sides of 9" glass pie pan, reserving 3 tablespoons of mixture. Place remaining mixture in separate pan. Toast in oven, along with pie shell, about 5 minutes. For filling: beat sour cream; add salt, 4 tablespoons of confectioners' sugar, orange juice, rind and vanilla. Spread on bottom and sides of shell. Cover with peaches, attractively arranged. Whip cream. Fold in remaining 2 tablespoons confectioners' sugar. Cover peaches with whipped cream and sprinkle with reserved crumbs. Chill.
Yield: 9" pie

Senator & Mrs. Abraham Ribicoff
Cornwall Bridge

Jody's Sinful Strawberry Pie

This is a rich and beautiful way to serve strawberries from Ellsworth Farm and other "pick your own" fields.

For crust:
1 cup flour
3 tablespoons confectioners' sugar
$^1/_2$ cup butter (no substitute)
For filling:
8 ounces cream cheese

$^1/_2$ cup sugar
Juice of $^1/_2$ large lemon
$^1/_2$ pint whipping cream, whipped
$1^1/_2$-2 pints fresh strawberries
6 ounces currant jelly

Preheat oven to 350°. For crust, mix flour and sugar, cut in butter to make crumbs. Pat into ungreased 10" glass pie pan. Bake 15 minutes until pale gold. For filling, mix softened cream cheese, sugar and lemon juice. Fold in whipped cream. Pour into cooled pie shell. Top with strawberries, bottoms up, largest berries in center. Melt jelly in saucepan over low heat. Stir until smooth. Drizzle jelly from teaspoon to cover each berry. Refrigerate 2 hours before serving.
8 Servings

George-Ann Gowan, Kent School
Kent

Mixed Berries
with Crème Anglaise and Raspberry Sauce

A beautiful summer recipe using local berries. Use an assortment of fresh blueberries, currants, raspberries, blackberries and halved strawberries.

For sauce:
2 12-ounce bags frozen
    unsweetened raspberries,
    thawed
6 tablespoons sugar
2 tablespoons Grand Marnier or
    other orange liqueur
For Creme Anglaise:
2^1/$_2$ cups half and half

1 vanilla bean, split lengthwise
6 egg yolks
^{3}/$_4$ cup sugar
1^1/$_2$ teaspoons cornstarch
2 tablespoons Cognac
Berries:
8 cups assorted berries
Mint sprigs for garnish

Make sauce: purée raspberries in processor. Strain through sieve, pressing on seeds. Mix sugar and Grand Marnier into purée. Cover and refrigerate. Make Crème Anglaise: place half and half in heavy medium saucepan. Scrape in seeds from vanilla bean; add bean. Bring to simmer. Whisk yolks, sugar and cornstarch in medium bowl to blend. Gradually whisk in hot half and half mixture. Return mixture to saucepan and stir over medium heat until custard thickens and leaves path on back of spoon when finger is drawn across, about 6 minutes. Strain into bowl. Mix in Cognac. Cover and refrigerate until well chilled. To serve, ladle both sauces onto each plate. Mound berries in center. Garnish with mint sprigs.
10 Servings

Nancy Fyfield
New Milford

Gingered Applesauce

Cider, spices and shredded ginger elevate this applesauce from the ordinary.

10 tart apples, peeled, cored and
    chopped
1^1/$_2$ cups cider
1 cinnamon stick

1 heaping tablespoon fresh ginger,
    shredded
^{1}/$_2$ teaspoon ground cloves
^{1}/$_2$ teaspoon nutmeg

Place all ingredients in a pot and bring to a boil. Cook uncovered over moderate heat for ^{1}/$_2$ hour.

Elaine Pratt
Bridgewater

Deep Dish Autumn Pie

This recipe is from my cookbook, "Fresh", which was inspired by the bounty of the Litchfield Hills. The apples (Cortlands are a favorite), pears and red grapes give this a luscious fall flavor.

Pastry for 9" double crust pie
4 cups cooking apples, pared and
   sliced
4 cups firm pears, pared and
   sliced
3 teaspoons lemon juice
2 cups seedless red grapes, halved
$^1/_2$ cup brown sugar, packed
$^1/_3$ cup granulated sugar

2 tablespoons flour
Pinch of salt
1 teaspoon grated lemon rind
1 teaspoon cinnamon
$^1/_2$ teaspoon nutmeg
1 tablespoon butter
1 egg, lightly beaten
Cinnamon sugar
Optional: vanilla ice cream

Preheat oven to 425°. Mix apples and pears and sprinkle with lemon juice. Add grapes and toss. Blend together next 7 ingredients. Toss with fruit and pour into greased 9"x15" baking dish. Dot with butter. Roll half the pastry to $^1/_4$" thickness until at least 1" wider than pan in all directions. Place gently over fruit, overlapping dish on all sides. Trim so that pastry slightly overhangs dish. Flute edges, make slits to allow steam to escape, and brush crust with beaten egg. Make cinnamon sugar using 1 part cinnamon to 3 parts sugar. Sprinkle on pie and bake for 35 minutes, or until crust is golden brown. Serve warm, with ice cream if desired.
8-10 Servings

Carol Schneider
Cornwall Bridge

Quince Candy

Quinces
Sugar

Cinnamon
Cloves, ground

Wipe off fuzz from quinces. Cover fruit with water and bring to boil. Boil briefly until soft. Drain and put through foodmill. Mix 3 measures quince to 2 measures sugar. Add cinnamon and cloves to taste. Bring to boil stirring constantly and continue boiling and stirring until mixture gets very thick and changes color to deep red (about one hour). Pour onto platters keeping mixture about 1" thick and let dry about 1 week. Turn over, put on clean platter. Let dry again. Keeps in tins between sheets of waxpaper up to 6 months. Serve in bite-size pieces.

Lisl Standen
South Kent

Fresh Fruit Pizza

These pizzas are beautiful and they're fun for adult or kid's parties.

1 cup warm water
1 tablespoon dry yeast
1 teaspoon salt
1 tablespoon sugar
2 cups flour (enough to make soft dough)

A mix of apples, pears, peaches, apricots or plums
$3/4$ cup white sugar
1 teaspoon cinnamon
$1/4$ teaspoon ground ginger
1 tablespoon all-purpose flour

Place first 4 ingredients in bowl and stir until yeast is dissolved. Slowly add flour until a kneadable dough is formed and can be turned out on floured surface. Knead 5 minutes. Cover dough and rest 20 minutes. Preheat oven to 375°. Meanwhile, peel, core and slice fruit. Mix together sugar, cinnamon, ginger, and 1 tablespoon flour. When dough is ready, oil cookie sheet and gently pick up dough ball, flip over in oil and with oily hands press dough out into large round about $1/2$" thick. Arrange fruit over dough and evenly sprinkle on sugar mixture. Bake approximately 20 minutes or until golden and bubbly. Serve warm.
6 Servings

Dana Jennings Rohn
Goshen

Mother's Apple Cake

This family recipe once won a prize from "The New Milford Times."

1 cup oil
$1^1/2$ cups sugar
3 eggs
2 cups all-purpose flour
1 teaspoon baking soda
1 teaspoon cinnamon

$1/2$ teaspoon salt
3 MacIntosh apples, thinly sliced
$1/2$ cup chopped nuts, divided
For topping:
1 tablespoon sugar
$1/2$ teaspoon cinnamon

Preheat oven to 375°. Combine oil, $1^1/2$ cups sugar, eggs and beat well. Sift dry ingredients into mixture and beat until creamy. Add apples and $1/4$ cup nuts. Beat well. Mix topping ingredients with remaining $1/4$ cup nuts. Pour batter into ungreased 10" tube pan. Sprinkle on topping mixture. Bake 45 to 50 minutes or until done.
10 Servings

Judith Tabacinski
New Milford

Rose Cream with Raspberries and Rose Petals

Roses have a very haunting, evocative flavor which I first tasted as a child in Syria. Purchase rose water at a specialty food store. For the garnish use local, unsprayed roses. The red to pale pink hues have the most perfume.

2¹/₂ cups heavy cream
¹/₂ cup milk
¹/₂ cup granulated sugar
3 whole eggs
4 egg yolks
1 tablespoon rose water
1¹/₂ teaspoons pure vanilla extract

For sauce:
1¹/₂ pints fresh raspberries
¹/₂ cup granulated sugar
1 tablespoon rose water
Juice of ¹/₂ fresh lemon
Garnish: fresh rose petals, rinsed

Preheat oven to 325°. Heat cream with milk and sugar in medium enameled saucepan over low heat, to just below boiling point. Stirring occasionally, dissolve sugar completely. Remove from heat and set aside. Place whole eggs, yolks and rose water in medium bowl and beat with whisk until incorporated. Stir in hot cream slowly, whisking constantly. Return cream to saucepan; whisk constantly over low heat until mixture coats spoon. Remove from heat, add vanilla extract and pour through fine strainer into a buttered 9" soufflé dish. Place dish into larger pan. Pour boiling water to reach ¹/₂ way up sides of dish. Place uncovered in center of oven. Bake 30-40 minutes. When done center of cream should be just set, but still tremble. Do not overcook or cream will separate. Remove from water bath. Cool, chill until completely cold, a few hours, or overnight. Make sauce: place berries in food processor with sugar, rose water and lemon juice. Purée until completely smooth. Pour through fine strainer to remove seeds. Cover sauce. Chill but serve at room temperature so sauce is fragrant. To serve, spoon pool of raspberry sauce on plate, place spoonful of rose cream on top and strew with rose petals.
8 Servings

Lynnia Milliun
Washington

Janice's Blueberry Cream Pie

Delicious, easy and impressive. For July 4th gatherings, add some strawberries on top.

1 deep dish 9" pie crust, baked
$^3/_4$ cup sugar
$^1/_4$ teaspoon salt
2 cups heavy cream or whipping cream
2 tablespoons butter

2 tablespoons confectioners' sugar
$^2/_3$ cup water
$2^1/_2$ tablespoons cornstarch
2 pints fresh blueberries, divided
$1^1/_2$ tablespoons lemon juice
$^1/_2$ teaspoon vanilla

Combine sugar, cornstarch and salt. Stir in water and 1 cup blueberries and bring to boil. Cook, stirring constantly until very thick, about 8 minutes. Stir in butter and lemon juice. Cool mixture. Reserving some for garnish, fold in remaining blueberries. Chill 1 hour. Beat cream until thick, add sugar and vanilla. Spread $^1/_2$ whipped cream on pie shell; top with blueberry mixture; spread rest of whipped cream over top. Garnish with remaining berries. Chill.
8 Servings

Janice Dobson
New Milford

Strawberry-Cassis Sherbet

Fast, easy, beautiful and perfect for those on low-cholesterol diets who still have a gluttonous appetite for sweets. The texture is best when made a few hours before serving.

2 12-ounce frozen unsweetened strawberries, half-thawed, or equal amount fresh
$^1/_4$ to $^1/_2$ cup honey
1 cup dry red wine

4 ounces cassis liqueur
1 tablespoon lemon juice or to taste
Candied violets

Purée all ingredients in food processor. Put purée in ice cream maker and freeze according to instructions. Garnish each individual scoop with candied violets and a big splash of cassis.
8 Servings

Francine du Plessix Gray
Warren

Mile High Pie

This easy dessert is luscious made with local berries.

1 baked pie shell
1-2 egg whites
1^1/$_2$ cups fresh sliced strawberries
    or raspberries

1 cup granulated sugar
1 cup heavy cream
Sliced bananas for garnish

In medium mixing bowl beat egg whites until stiff. Slowly add sugar and fruit while beating. Mixture should fill ^{3}/$_4$ or more of the bowl. Whip cream. Fold cream into mixture. Pour into pie shell. Place in freezer. Try not to freeze too hard. Garnish with sliced bananas.
6-8 Servings

Peter Pratt
Bridgewater

Fourth of July Pavlova

In Australia, from whence I hail, this dessert is filled with tropical fruits. Here I make it like a flag for Independence Day — using blueberry stars and raspberry stripes. My father-in-law, Skitch Henderson, loves it.

4 large egg whites
Pinch of salt
1^1/$_4$ cups superfine sugar
^{1}/$_2$ teaspoon vanilla
1 teaspoon lemon juice

1 tablespoon cornstarch
1 pint whipping cream
2 tablespoons superfine sugar
1 pint blueberries or blackberries
2 pints red raspberries

Preheat oven to 300°. With electric beater, beat egg whites with salt until soft peaks form. Continue to beat, gradually adding sugar, vanilla and lemon juice until stiff, 5-6 minutes. Fold in the cornstarch with spatula. Line baking sheet with parchment paper. Spread half the batter onto paper, making a rectangle at least ^{1}/$_2$" thick. Use remaining meringue to build up sides of rectangle so it has a slight edge. Place in oven, reduce heat to 250°, and bake 1^1/$_2$ hours until puffed and slightly browned. Turn off oven. Let meringue cool 1 hour before removing. (It will crack a little.) Carefully remove parchment paper and place meringue on serving plate. Whip cream with 2 tablespoons superfine sugar. Fill meringue with whipped cream. Arrange blueberries in upper left corner for stars, and use raspberries for stripes.
10-12 Servings

Sandra Watson
New Milford

Burgundy Poached Pears with Dark Chocolate Sauce

This recipe celebrates our wonderful orchards and wineries and chocolate is always a hit. It's a cozy dessert for cool evenings and looks beautiful.

6 firm pears with stems	Chocolate Sauce:
2 cups Burgundy wine	1 pint heavy cream
1 cup granulated sugar	12 ounces dark chocolate,
2 cinnamon sticks	chopped
2 tablespoons lemon juice	$1/2$ cup brandy
1 teaspoon allspice	Whipped cream

Peel pears, leaving stem intact, and remove core from bottom. Place in large saucepan with wine, sugar, cinnamon sticks, lemon juice and allspice; simmer until tender. Allow to cool in wine. Make chocolate sauce. Bring heavy cream to boil in medium saucepan, being careful not to boil over. Add chocolate and stir until chocolate is melted. Add brandy and remove from heat. Remove pear from wine and stand on plate. Spoon some of warm chocolate sauce over pear, allowing it to run down and pool. Garnish with whipped cream and pass additional chocolate sauce.
6 Servings

Ruedi Hauser, Hauser Chocolatier
Bethel

Banana Pear Compote

Water	Fresh pears
Sugar	Bananas
Juice from fresh lemon	Chopped walnuts

Boil equal amount of sugar and water to make syrup. Flavor with lemon juice and cool. Just prior to serving, slice fruit, sprinkle with nuts and pour syrup over all.

John Richardson
New Milford

French Apple Tart Patsy

A light, not too sweet, year-round dessert. It's no more difficult than apple pie, but the three layers make it look impressive.

For crust:
5 tablespoons butter, room
    temperature
$^1/_2$ cup granulated sugar
1 large egg
1 teaspoon vanilla
$1^1/_4$ cups all-purpose flour
Bread or cake crumbs
For apples:
3-4 firm cooking apples, peeled,
    cored and thickly sliced

$^1/_2$ cup sugar
$^1/_2$ cup water
For brandy cream:
$^1/_3$ cup sugar
$^1/_4$ cup flour
1 egg
$^3/_4$ cup heavy cream
$^1/_4$ cup brandy
For garnish:
Confectioners' sugar

Mix crust ingredients together and let rest $^1/_2$ hour. Preheat oven to 375°. Roll out crust to fit 9" tart pan with removable bottom. Prick crust with fork and bake until firm to touch but not brown. Cool. Sprinkle bottom with crumbs. Cook apples gently in sugar and water. Drain. Overlap slices in tart shell in nice pattern. Bake 10 minutes. Remove from oven. Whisk brandy cream ingredients until smooth. Almost cover apple layer with brandy cream and return to oven until cream is set, but not brown. Sprinkle with confectioners' sugar and return to oven until tart is as brown as you wish. Serve warm or cold.
6-8 Servings

**Patsy Stroble, The Stroble Baking Company
Kent**

Blueberry Upside-Down Cake

My aunt gave me this yummy recipe.

1 pint fresh blueberries
$^3/_4$ cup sugar, divided
$^1/_4$ cup shortening
1 egg
1 cup flour

$1^1/_2$ teaspoons baking powder
$^1/_8$ teaspoon salt
$^1/_2$ cup milk
Whipped cream

Preheat oven to 375°. Place washed blueberries into buttered $1^1/_2$ quart casserole and sprinkle with $^1/_4$ cup sugar. In bowl, cream shortening, remaining sugar and egg together. Sift flour, baking powder and salt together. Add this alternately with milk to creamed mixture. Pour on top of berries. Bake for 45 minutes. Spoon out and top with whipped cream.
4-6 Servings

**June Wildberger
New Milford**

Connecticut Yankee Strawberry Rhubarb Pie

Pastry for double crust 9" pie:
1¹/₂ cups sugar
¹/₄ cup all-purpose flour
¹/₄ teaspoon salt
¹/₄ teaspoon grated fresh
   Connecticut nutmeg

3 cups Connecticut rhubarb, cut in
   ¹/₂" pieces
1 cup Connecticut strawberries,
   sliced
1 tablespoon butter

Preheat oven to 400°. Line 9" pie plate with ¹/₂ of pastry, prick with fork and partially bake, 7 minutes. Mix dry ingredients and set aside. Combine strawberries and rhubarb, add to flour mixture. Mix well and let stand 20 minutes. When ready, pour into baked pastry shell. Dot with butter. With remaining pastry, cover fruit with well-pricked top or lattice. Bake 40-45 minutes.

Senator Christopher J. Dodd
Wethersfield

Pegge's Raspberry Lemon Cheesecake

Every summer we pick our raspberries at the farm next to the 1741 Salt-box Inn in Sherman. They grow at least three varieties and their berries are orbits above the little boxes of berries from Chile.

For crust:
1 cup all-purpose white flour
2 tablespoons sugar
¹/₂ cup butter
1 jumbo egg yolk
1 teaspoon vanilla extract
For filling:
1¹/₂ pounds cream cheese,
   softened

1 pound farmers' cheese
2 tablespoons grated lemon peel
1³/₄ cups sugar
3 tablespoons all-purpose flour
5 jumbo eggs
2 jumbo egg yolks
For topping:
4 tablespoons raspberry jam
1 pint raspberries

Make crust: preheat oven to 400°. In food processor, blend flour and butter until it looks like bread crumbs, add yolk and vanilla and process until it forms a ball of dough. Use ¹/₂ of dough to press onto base of ungreased 10" springform pan. Bake the bottom for 10-15 minutes until brown. Attach side of pan, and press remaining dough on sides of pan. Set aside. Increase oven to 475° . Make filling: combine all ingredients in processor bowl. (It will be full, but it does fit!) After mix has blended, process 2 minutes. Pour filling into springform pan; bake 10-15 minutes. Reduce heat to 200° and bake 1¹/₂ hours or longer until cake has set. Turn off heat, keeping cake in oven with door ajar, 30 minutes. Cool on rack, then chill overnight. Brush warm jam on top and garnish with berries.
8-10 Servings

Pegge Patterson
New Milford

New England Apple Cake

This cake is luscious made with local apples and served with steaming hot coffee. It can be stored 2 days at room temperature and up to two weeks in refrigerator.

2 eggs
2 cups sugar
1 cup vegetable oil
1 teaspoon vanilla
2 cups all-purpose flour
2 teaspoons cinnamon
$^1/_2$ teaspoon salt

1 teaspoon baking soda
$1^1/_2$ teaspoons water
1 cup chopped walnuts
4 cups apples, peeled, cored and
    coarsely chopped
2 tablespoons confectioners' sugar

Preheat oven to 350°. In large bowl, beat together eggs, sugar, oil and vanilla until smooth. Blend together flour, cinnamon and salt. Add flour mixture to egg mixture, blending well. Dissolve baking soda in water. Add to batter and combine well. Add nuts and apples, combine well (batter will be thick). Spoon batter into greased 9"x13" baking pan. Bake 55 minutes or until toothpick comes out clean. When completely cooled, dust with sugar.

Judy C. Williams
New Milford

Summer Pudding with Cherries

In England, where I grew up, this dish meant summer. It still does. Living in the Litchfield Hills I have discovered many more fruits to use. The fun is the combinations. It's better made the day before.

$^1/_2$ pound red or black currants
$^3/_4$ pound cherries, pitted
$^1/_2$ pound raspberries, or other
    fresh fruits

$^1/_4$ pint water
4-6 ounces sugar
Thinly sliced, firm white bread
Heavy cream

Wash fruit and stew with sugar and a little water. Cool. Take crusts off bread and cut each slice in half lengthwise. Line sides of pudding bowl or soufflé dish with bread. Cover bottom of dish with triangles of bread. Trim bread at top edge of bowl. There must not be any holes. Fill dish with fruit mixture. Cut more bread triangles and cover top. Place a flat plate on pudding. Put a weight (about 2 pounds) on plate and chill overnight in refrigerator. Turn out onto serving dish. Pour on any remaining juice and serve with heavy cream.
6-8 Servings

Joanna Gitterman
South Kent

Fresh Citrus Jelly

This old family recipe makes a light, refreshing finale when garnished with whipped cream and mint leaves.

1 envelope Knox gelatin
²/₃ cup sugar
Juice of one lemon

1¹/₄ cups fresh orange juice
Sweetened whipped cream
Mint leaves

Soak gelatin in ¹/₃ cup cold water. Bring ¹/₂ cup water to boil. Dissolve gelatin in it until clear. Add sugar, lemon juice and orange juice. Put in 4 greased molds or custard cups. Chill until set, 2-3 hours. Garnish.
4-5 Servings

Mrs. George A. Murphy
Washington

Mystery Sorbet

Nobody will guess what the ingredients are!

1 cup sugar
1 cup water
2-3 pears, peeled and cored
1¹/₂-2 cucumbers, peeled and
  seeded

Fresh mint leaves
Fresh lemon juice

Make syrup by boiling sugar and water. Slice pears, cucumbers and mint leaves to taste into food processor. Process thoroughly and pour with the sugar syrup and a squeeze of lemon into an ice cream or sherbert machine. Freeze according to instructions.
4 Servings

John Richardson
New Milford

Ending on a high note

transcendent desserts destined
to charm everyone from 4th of July revelers to
romantic hilltop stargazers---and guests at
your own special celebrations at home.

Chocolate Orange Marble Cake

This is a great cake for a picnic. It tastes even better if refrigerated a day before serving.

1 cup butter, softened
1^1/$_4$ cups sugar, divided
3 egg yolks
1^3/$_4$ cups flour
^{3}/$_4$ teaspoon baking powder
^{3}/$_4$ teaspoon baking soda

1 cup sour cream
2 ounces unsweetened chocolate, melted
Grated rind of one orange
2 egg whites
^{1}/$_2$ cup orange juice

Preheat oven to 350°. In large bowl, cream together butter and one cup sugar until light. Add yolks one at a time. Sift together flour, baking powder and soda; add this to butter mixture alternately with sour cream. Beat until smooth. Divide between two bowls. Into one, stir grated rind and into other, stir chocolate. In another bowl, beat whites to stiff peaks. Fold half the whites into each of the batters. Butter and line with buttered wax paper, a 6"x10" loaf, or 9" square pan. Pour in both batters. Swirl to marbleize. Bake 70 minutes. Cool in pan five minutes. Combine orange juice with remaining ^{1}/$_4$ cup sugar and pour slowly over cake. Let cake cool completely, invert onto rack and discard waxed paper.

Heather Herstatt
New Milford

Willie's Brownies

This recipe makes the best brownies I have ever eaten. They're easy and have a perfect consistency, chewy, yet cake-like, moist and chocolatey.

9 ounces best quality bittersweet chocolate
^{1}/$_2$ pound butter
3 cups sugar
6 eggs

1 tablespoon vanilla
1^1/$_2$ cups flour
1 teaspoon salt
1^1/$_2$ cups chopped nuts

Preheat oven to 350°. Melt chocolate over hot water. Let cool. Beat softened butter with sugar until mixed. Add eggs, one at a time. Add chocolate and vanilla until blended. Add flour and salt. Stir, add nuts. Pour into greased 11"x16" pan. Place on center rack in oven and bake 20-25 minutes or until center is done. Cut into squares when cool. Store wrapped in plastic, or freeze in foil.
Yield: 40 squares

Darla Karlton, The Dam Caterers
Roxbury

Caramel Pot de Crème

This is a delicious dessert served at our restaurant. Garnish with chocolate biscotti or almond lace cookies.

2 cups sugar
$^1/_2$ cup water
12 egg yolks

1 quart heavy cream
2 cups milk

Caramelize 2 cups sugar with $^1/_2$ cup water — watch closely and do not let sugar get dark. Whisk 12 egg yolks. Boil 1 quart heavy cream and 2 cups milk — slowly add to sugar mixture. Slowly add milk mixture to egg yolks. Strain and cool to room temperature. Skim froth from top. Preheat oven to 300°. Pour into 8-ounce custard cups. Place cups in baking pan. Cook in waterbath 50 minutes.
12 Servings

Elissa G.T. Potts, The Fife and Drum Restaurant and Inn
Kent

Toasted Hazelnut Macaroons

These make a lovely holiday gift.

4 cups hazelnuts
1 cup sugar

4 large egg whites

Preheat broiler. Put hazelnuts on heavy-gauge cookie sheet with rim. Broil 4" from heat, turning frequently with a large kitchen spoon, until skins are dry, uniformly dark and nuts are toasted. Watch carefully to avoid burning. Turn into sieve, a cup at a time, and shake to remove skins. Cool. Preheat oven to 300°. Grind nuts finely in food processor. Turn into medium bowl. Combine thoroughly with egg whites and sugar to make paste. Spread dough on a well greased 12"x15" cookie sheet with rim to within $^1/_2$" of rim; dough will expand. Bake 10 minutes; reduce heat to 200° and continue baking for another 10 minutes. Remove from oven. Cut into $1^1/_2$" squares. Cookies should be crusty outside and soft inside. Store in air-tight container.
Yield: 80 cookies

Greti Hediger
New Milford

Brandy Apricot-Almond Torte

For pastry:
1²/₃ cups all-purpose flour
2 tablespoons sugar
1 egg yolk
¹/₂ cup unsalted butter, chilled,
    cut into pieces
4 teaspoons cold water

For filling:
2 cups dried apricots, chopped
¹/₂ cup brandy
1 cup unsalted butter, melted
1¹/₂ cups sugar
4 large eggs
2 cups sliced almonds

Make pastry: blend flour and sugar in food processor. Add butter and cut in using on/off turns until mixture resembles coarse meal. Blend in egg yolk and enough water by tablespoon to bind dough. Gather dough into ball, then flatten into disk. Wrap in plastic, chill 30 minutes. Roll dough out on lightly floured surface to ¹/₄" thick round. Press dough onto bottom and about 2" up sides of 9"x2¹/₂" springform pan. Refrigerate. Make filling: soak apricots in brandy for 45 minutes to 1 hour. Drain; reserve brandy. Preheat oven to 350°. Whisk in brandy and eggs. Mix in almonds. Sprinkle apricots over dough. Pour almond mixture over apricots. Bake about 1¹/₄ hours or until filling no longer moves in the center when pan is shaken and the top is brown, (cover with foil if top becomes very brown). Cool about 30 minutes. Loosen and remove from pan. Allow to cool completely. Serve with whipped cream.
8 Servings

The Boulders Inn
New Preston

Tigger's Pecan Pie

1 9" pie crust, unbaked
1 cup large pecan halves, divided
2 large eggs, beaten
²/₃ cup brown sugar

1 cup light corn syrup
¹/₂ teaspoon vanilla
1 rounded tablespoon butter,
    melted

Preheat oven to 375°. In a mini-food processor, grind ¹/₃ cup pecans until paste is formed. Transfer to medium bowl, beat in eggs; add sugar, syrup, vanilla and butter. Beat until smooth. Stir in remaining pecans, pour into pie shell. Bake for 35-40 minutes until filling is set.
8 Servings

Tigger Peterson
New Milford

Hartford Election Cake

In New England, town meetings were held in March and often lasted all day. During the noon recess, the colonists would go to the village store to eat March Meeting or 'Lection Cake. Later in Hartford, these cakes were eaten while awaiting the returns.

2³/₄ cups all-purpose flour, divided
1 package active dry yeast
¹/₄ teaspoon salt
¹/₄ teaspoon ground nutmeg
1 cup milk

¹/₃ cup granulated sugar
¹/₄ cup brown sugar, packed
¹/₄ cup butter
1 large egg
1 cup raisins

Preheat oven to 350°. In large mixing bowl combine 1 cup of the flour, yeast, salt and nutmeg. In saucepan, heat milk, sugars and butter just until warm (115-120°), stirring constantly. Add to dry mixture in bowl, add egg; beat on low speed of electric mixer for ¹/₂ minute. Scrape side of bowl constantly. Beat 3 minutes at high speed. By hand, stir in remaining flour and raisins. Cover. Let rise in warm place until doubled (about 1¹/₂ hours). Stir dough down. Spoon into greased loaf pan. Let rise until nearly double (about 1 hour). Bake 40 minutes. Makes one loaf.
8-12 Servings

Frank Benham, Morey's IGA
New Milford

Chocolate Mayonnaise Cake

This cake is a staple at fairs and bake sales throughout Litchfield County.

2 cups sifted all-purpose flour
1¹/₂ teaspoons baking soda
¹/₄ teaspoon salt
4 tablespoons sifted unsweetened cocoa

1 cup good quality mayonnaise
1 cup granulated sugar
1 cup cold water
1 teaspoon vanilla extract
Your favorite frosting (optional)

Preheat oven to 350°. Grease and flour 9" square pan or 11³/₄" x7¹/₂" sheet pan. Sift together flour, baking soda, salt and cocoa. Set aside. In large bowl of electric mixer, beat together mayonnaise and sugar. On lowest speed, alternately add flour mixture and water to batter, beating after each addition, beginning and ending with flour. Stir in vanilla, beat 2 minutes longer. Turn into pan. Smooth level, then spread slightly from center toward edges of pan so it will rise evenly. Bake 35-40 minutes, or until cake tester comes out clean. Cool on wire rack 10 minutes; remove from pan. Frost if desired.
12 Servings

Norma Went
Roxbury

Grandmother's Date Squares

This family recipe dates back to 1887 in Moosic, PA. We always had large jars of these squares in our big country kitchen and washed them down with strong tea from the back of the old fashioned stove.

2 cups pitted dates
1 cup sugar
$^1/_2$ cup water
3 tablespoons flour
2 cups quick oats

2 cups flour
1 teaspoon salt
1 teaspoon baking soda
1 cup brown sugar
1 cup melted butter

Mix first 4 ingredients in top of double boiler. Cook until thick and then cool. Preheat oven to 350°. In large bowl, mix oats, 2 cups of flour, salt, baking soda, brown sugar and butter. Crumble mixture with hands. Pat half of crumbs in bottom of greased 9"x13" pan. Spread date mixture over top and cover with remaining crumb mixture. Bake 30 minutes. When cool cut into squares.
Yield: 40 squares

David Eugene Bell
Washington Depot

Brownie Cupcakes

I bring these to Northville School to celebrate teachers' birthdays. Children and adults love them. Great for picnics.

1 cup butter
$^1/_2$ cup chocolate bits
$1^1/_2$ cups chopped walnuts or
    pecans
$1^1/_4$ cups unsifted all-purpose
    flour

$^1/_4$ teaspoon salt
$1^1/_2$ cups sugar
4 eggs, beaten
$^1/_4$ teaspoon vanilla extract

Preheat oven to 325°. Line cupcake pans with 21 papers. Melt butter and chocolate bits over very low heat, stirring. Stir in chopped nuts. Set aside. Sift together into large bowl: flour, salt and sugar. Add eggs and vanilla extract. Stir in chocolate mixture and mix well. Fill cups about $^2/_3$ full and bake for 25-30 minutes. Cool. Leave plain, sprinkle with confectioners' sugar or frost.
Yield: 21 cupcakes

Pamela Collins
New Milford

Carrot Cake with Walnuts and Currants

This recipe came with the former Milk Pail Restaurant when we bought it in 1978, and it's still a favorite. Serve it plain with ice cream or frost with cream cheese or lemon frosting.

1¼ cups oil
4 cups grated carrots
2½ cups flour
2½ cups sugar
1½ teaspoons baking powder
1½ teaspoons baking soda

2 teaspoons cinnamon
1 teaspoon salt
1 cup chopped pecans or walnuts
1 cup currants
4 eggs
½ cup water

Preheat oven to 350°. In small bowl, pour oil over carrots and set aside. In large bowl, stir together next 8 ingredients. Add eggs and water, then carrot-oil mixture. Stir to blend well. Pour into greased tube pan, bake 40-50 minutes. Cake should be firm to touch and pulling away from sides of pan.
16 Servings

Penny L. Schmutzler
Kent

Decadent Chocolate Soufflé Cake

Because this quick and easy cake is leavened only with egg whites, the center may fall slightly. Simply fill it with fresh berries, then dust with sugar.

10 ounces semisweet chocolate
1 stick + 2 tablespoons sweet
  butter
3 tablespoons flour
5 eggs, separated

½ cup + 2 tablespoons sugar,
  divided
⅛ teaspoon salt
Fresh berries
Confectioners' sugar

Preheat oven to 350°. Grease and flour 9" pan. In top of double boiler over simmering water, melt chocolate and butter, stirring until smooth. Whisk in flour, approximately half the sugar and the egg yolks. In mixing bowl, whip the egg whites until foamy, 10-15 seconds. Add salt and continue beating until soft peaks form, gradually adding remaining sugar to form a meringue. Fold meringue mixture quickly and thoroughly into egg yolk mixture. Pour batter into prepared cake pan and bake 30-35 minutes until center is set. Cool slightly in pan, turn out onto a serving platter and dust generously with confectioners' sugar before serving. May be frozen.
8 Servings

Linda Melone, Linda's Desserts
Danbury

Toasted Oatmeal Cookies

These cookies are good for you. They actually have negative calories. Even in our healthy Litchfield Hills environment, everyone needs a negative calorie cookie once in a while.

$3/4$ cup butter
$2^1/2$ cups oats
$3/4$ cup whole wheat flour
$1/2$ teaspoon salt
$1/2$ teaspoon baking powder

$2/3$ cup honey
1 egg
1 teaspoon vanilla
$1/2$ cup raisins
$1/2$ cup toasted slivered almonds

In a skillet, melt butter. Add oats, toasting until golden brown. Preheat oven to 350°. Stir flour, salt and baking powder together in mixing bowl. Add honey, egg and vanilla to dry mixture. Add cooled oats and mix. Add raisins and toasted slivered almonds. Drop by teaspoons on ungreased baking sheet. Bake 10-12 minutes. Dough stays fresh in refrigerator 2-3 days or may be frozen.

Ellen Shrader and Ed Witkin
Bridgewater

Thea Mary's Proxamaria Cookies

These not-too-sweet Greek cookies from my friend's Thea (Aunt) Mary are a snap to make. Good with coffee or hot chocolate on a snowy day.

$1/4$ pound butter at room
    temperature
2 tablespoons shortening
1 cup sugar
3 eggs, separated
1 teaspoon vanilla

3 cups flour
1 teaspoon baking powder
$1/2$ teaspoon baking soda
1 egg yolk, beaten
Sesame seeds

Preheat oven to 350°. Cream butter, shortening and sugar well. Add egg yolks one at a time, and add vanilla. Whip egg whites until stiff. Fold into butter mixture. Blend dry ingredients. Add to butter/egg mixture. Knead until smooth. Divide in half. Shape into loaves no more than $1/2$" thick. Place on greased cookie sheet. Brush with remaining egg yolk and sprinkle with sesame seeds. Bake at 350° for 20 minutes. Immediately slice and toast lightly. Store in airtight container.
Yield: 3-4 dozen

Cheryl Pyers
New Milford

Microwave Mississippi Mud Cake

A true picnic dessert, loved by kids and adults alike. I always take it to our July 4th gathering at Shepaug High School.

For cake:
1 cup butter
2 cups granulated sugar
$^1/_2$ cup unsweetened cocoa
    powder
4 large eggs
2 teaspoons vanilla extract
1$^1/_2$ cups all-purpose flour
$^1/_4$ cup walnuts, coarsely chopped

$^1/_4$ teaspoon salt
4 ounces miniature marshmallows
For frosting:
$^1/_2$ cup butter
$^1/_3$ cup milk
$^1/_4$ cup unsweetened cocoa
    powder
$^1/_2$ teaspoon vanilla extract
1 box confectioners' sugar

Make cake: Put butter in large non-metal mixing bowl. Microwave on high 1-1$^1/_2$ minutes until melted. Stir in sugar and cocoa powder. Add eggs and vanilla, beat vigorously until well blended. Stir in flour, walnuts and salt. Let batter rest 10 minutes. Pour into 8"x13" glass baking dish. Place on a plastic trivet or inverted saucer in microwave. Microwave on medium, 9 minutes, rotating dish $^1/_2$ turn after 3 minutes. Shield the corners of the dish with small triangles of foil (don't let triangles touch each other or sides of oven). Microwave on high 3-5 minutes, rotating dish $^1/_2$ turn once, until top is mostly dry with a few moist spots and pick inserted near center comes out clean. Sprinkle marshmallows evenly over top of cake. Let stand about 5 minutes until marshmallows are slightly melted. To make frosting: put butter in large bowl. Microwave on high 30-60 seconds until melted. Stir in milk, cocoa powder, and vanilla. Add sugar, beat vigorously till smooth. Spread evenly over marshmallows. Let stand 30 minutes. Serve at room temperature.
16 Servings

Ashley Farmen, Rumsey Hall School
Washington Depot

Chocolate Oatmeal Drops

These are quick and easy no-bake cookies — delicious and nutritious!

2 cups sugar
2 tablespoons unsweetened cocoa
$^2/_3$ cup milk

3 cups quick cooking oats
1 teaspoon vanilla
$^1/_3$ cup chunky peanut butter

Combine sugar, cocoa and milk in a saucepan. Bring to a boil and boil for one minute. Remove from stove. Stir into the mixture the oats, vanilla and peanut butter. Mix well. Drop by teaspoon onto waxed paper and let set.
Yield: 4 dozen

**Joan Byrne
New Milford**

Dark Chocolate Cookies with White Chocolate Chunks

These simple-to-make cookies are very chocolatey, yet the white chocolate is never overpowered. They are a big hit with our customers when warm from the oven.

$^1/_2$ pound unsalted butter, at
    room temperature
$1^3/_4$ cups sugar
2 large eggs, at room temperature
$1^1/_2$ teaspoons vanilla extract
1 ounce unsweetened chocolate,
    melted
$^1/_4$ cup sour cream
$^3/_4$ pound white chocolate,
    coarsely chopped

$2^1/_2$ cups flour
1 cup unsweetened cocoa
    (preferably Dutch-process)
$^1/_2$ teaspoon baking soda
$^1/_2$ teaspoon baking powder
$^1/_2$ teaspoon salt
1 cup coarsely chopped walnuts
    or pecans

Preheat oven to 350°. Grease baking sheet or line with parchment paper. Using electric mixer cream butter and sugar together in large bowl until light and fluffy. Beat in eggs, one at a time. Blend in vanilla, unsweetened chocolate, and sour cream. Fold in white chocolate. In large bowl, sift together flour, cocoa, baking soda, baking powder and salt. Mix into butter mixture. Stir in nuts. Drop rounded tablespoons of the dough onto prepared sheet, spacing 2" apart. Bake until nearly firm but still soft to touch in center, about 10 minutes. Transfer cookies to wire racks to cool. Store in airtight container at room temperature.
Yield: 6 Dozen

**Sandra Champlain, Kent Coffee and Chocolate Company
Kent**

Coffee Biscuit Tortoni

This is an easy, elegant, do-ahead dessert. It makes a grand finale to an Italian dinner.

1 cup heavy cream
$^1/_4$ cup sugar
1 tablespoon instant coffee
　　powder
1 teaspoon vanilla

1 egg white
2 tablespoons sugar
$^1/_2$ cup cookie crumbs
Chocolate sprinkles

Whip cream until almost stiff; fold in sugar, coffee powder and vanilla. Beat until stiff. With clean beaters, beat egg white until foamy; add 2 tablespoons of sugar and beat until stiff. Fold in crumbs, then fold egg white mixture into whipped cream. Spoon into 8 fluted paper or foil cups. Sprinkle more crumbs or chocolate sprinkles on top. Freeze until firm.
8 Servings

Pat Greenspan
New Milford

Mocha Toffee Bars

Nice with tea in front of the fire.

2 tablespoons instant espresso
　　powder
2 tablespoons boiling water
2 sticks unsalted butter, softened
1 cup brown sugar, firmly packed
1 large egg yolk

$1^1/_2$ teaspoons vanilla
$^1/_2$ teaspoon salt
2 cups all-purpose flour
8 ounces semisweet chocolate,
　　melted
$^1/_2$ cup salted cashews, chopped

Preheat oven to 350°. Dissolve espresso powder in boiling water. In bowl with electric mixer cream butter, add brown sugar and beat until light and fluffy. Beat in egg yolk, add vanilla and espresso mixture, beat until well combined. Add salt and flour, beating well. Spread batter evenly in a 15"x10"x1" pan and bake in middle of oven for 15-20 minutes or until it pulls away from edge of pan. Spread melted chocolate over baked layer and then sprinkle on cashews. Let cool in pan on a rack. Chill until chocolate is firm. Cut into bars.
48 Bars

Mrs. Earl F. Tasman
Sherman

1830 Clove Cake

This rich and delicious dessert is the favorite birthday cake in our family. It does not have (or need) a frosting but vanilla ice cream complements it nicely.

1 cup butter
2¹/₄ cups sugar
5 eggs
3 cups sifted flour
1 tablespoon ground cloves

1 tablespoon cinnamon
Pinch of salt
1 cup buttermilk or sour milk, divided
1 teaspoon baking soda

Preheat oven to 350°. Cream butter until soft. Add sugar gradually and continue beating until mixture is light and fluffy. In separate bowl beat eggs thoroughly. Add to creamed mixture, and blend thoroughly. Sift flour, cloves, cinnamon and salt. Add ¹/₃ of dry ingredients to batter. Mix. Stir in ¹/₂ cup buttermilk. Add another ¹/₃ of flour-spice combination and mix well. Stir baking soda into remaining ¹/₂ cup buttermilk, and mix into batter with remaining flour. Pour batter into greased 10" tube pan. Bake for 45-55 minutes or until cake tests done. Cool 10 minutes; turn out on rack. Best "aged" a day or two.
14-16 Servings

Diana Savory
Goshen

Frozen Lemon Mousse

This recipe from Ruth Gaynell is refreshing, easy and elegant.

6 eggs
1 cup sugar
8 tablespoons lemon juice

2¹/₂ cups vanilla wafer crumbs, divided
1 pint heavy cream

Separate eggs. Beat yolks. Add sugar and cook in double boiler until smooth (about 10 minutes). While mixture cooks, crush wafers. Line medium sized springform pan, greased with butter, with ¹/₂ of crumbs, saving remainder for top. Whip cream. Lightly fold into custard. Add lemon juice. Beat egg whites; fold into custard. Pour into pan; cover with remaining wafer crumbs. Place in freezer for at least 4 hours, put on serving plate; remove sides of pan. Let stand 10-15 minutes before serving.
12 Servings

Robert K. Darden
Sharon

Grandmother Scott's Lemon Meringue Pie

Longtime Bridgewater resident, Eleanor Gowan, shares her legendary pie recipe, which fetched $90.00 at a local charity auction.

For crust:
1 cup all-purpose flour
$1/2$ teaspoon salt
5 tablespoons Crisco
3 tablespoons soft butter
2-3 tablespoons ice water
For filling:
7 tablespoons cornstarch
$1^1/2$ cups sugar
$1/2$ teaspoon salt

2 cups boiling water
3 large egg yolks, lightly beaten
2 tablespoons butter
$1/2$ cup fresh lemon juice
1 tablespoon grated lemon rind
For meringue:
3 large egg whites, room
  temperature
6 tablespoons sugar

Preheat oven to 450°. Sift together flour and salt. Cut in shortening until particles are size of small peas. Add enough ice water to make a dough moist enough to hold together. Gather into ball and roll to $1/8$" thickness. Fit loosely in a 9" pie plate, patting out air pockets and trim 1" beyond rim to form edge. Prick lightly with small tined fork and bake 10-12 minutes, until golden. Cool on wire rack. Make filling: combine first 3 ingredients in top of double boiler. Add boiling water, stirring constantly to avoid lumps. When thickened, continue cooking over boiling water 20 minutes. Remove $1/2$ cup hot mixture and beat into egg yolks. Return to boiler, blending well, cook 2 minutes, stirring constantly. Remove from heat, blend in remaining three ingredients. Cool before turning into crust. Preheat oven to 425°. Beat egg whites until soft mounds form. Add sugar gradually, beating until stiff. Spread meringue gently over filling, sealing to edges. Bake 8-10 minutes until meringue peaks are golden brown.
8 Servings

Eleanor Gowan
Washington

Chocoholic's Cheesecake

This is easy, fast and a wonder to behold. It's chocolatey, creamy, but not overly cheesy. Best made one day ahead.

For cake:
12 ounces semi-sweet chocolate
3 tablespoons butter
1¹/₂ pounds cream cheese,
    softened
2 teaspoons vanilla
1¹/₂ cups whipping cream

1 cup sugar
4 eggs, beaten
3 tablespoons unsweetened cocoa
For crust:
1 package chocolate wafers
¹/₂ cup melted butter
1 teaspoon cinnamon

Melt chocolate and butter. Let cool. Make crust: crush wafers, add butter and cinnamon, mix well and press into 10" ungreased springform pan. Preheat oven to 350°. Beat cheese until fluffy, then beat in chocolate-butter mixture. Gradually add vanilla and whipping cream. Slowly add sugar and eggs. Add cocoa and mix well. Pour mixture into crust. Bake 30 minutes. Turn oven off and let stand in oven with door open slightly for 30 minutes. Remove from oven and cool at room temperature. Refrigerate overnight.
12-15 Servings

Judith Burroughs
New Milford

Salzburg Soufflé

2 egg yolks
1 teaspoon vanilla extract
¹/₂ teaspoon grated lemon peel
1 tablespoon flour

4 egg whites
2 tablespoons sugar
Confectioners' sugar

Preheat oven to 350°; beat egg yolks with fork and beat in vanilla and lemon peel; mix in flour. Beat egg whites until quite stiff, then add sugar and beat until whites are very stiff. Gently fold in egg yolk mixture. Butter oblong baking dish and add mixture in 3 mounds. Bake for 10 minutes; sprinkle with confectioners' sugar and serve immediately.

Lisl Standen
Kent

Index

More books!

Additional copies of
COOKING in the Litchfield Hills
may be purchased by contacting
The Pratt Center
163 Papermill Road
New Milford, CT 06776
(203) 355-3137
Cash, Checks, VISA and MasterCard
are accepted.
For the birthday cook. The weekend cook.
The holiday cook.

COOKING is the perfect gift.